CAMBRIDGE LIBRARY COLLECTION

Books of enduring scholarly value

British and Irish History, Nineteenth Century

This series comprises contemporary or near-contemporary accounts of the political, economic and social history of the British Isles during the nineteenth century. It includes material on international diplomacy and trade, labour relations and the women's movement, developments in education and social welfare, religious emancipation, the justice system, and special events including the Great Exhibition of 1851.

Baroness Burdett-Coutts

Granddaughter of the banker Thomas Coutts, the philanthropist Angela Georgina Burdett-Coutts (1814–1906) was one of the most remarkable women of her age, giving away an estimated £4 million of her inheritance to a wide range of causes. She set an example to others, offering practical support without fuss, and worked with Charles Dickens on schemes to improve the lot of the poverty-stricken. The Church of England was another beneficiary of her largesse, receiving endowments for bishoprics, churches and school buildings. The welfare of animals also deeply concerned her, and she was actively involved with the RSPCA. This anonymously compiled book, endorsed by her great friend Mary of Teck and published in 1893 for the international exposition in Chicago, presents a fascinating summary of her diverse charitable work. Burdett-Coutts herself edited for the exposition *Woman's Mission*, a series of papers on female philanthropy, also reissued in this series.

Cambridge University Press has long been a pioneer in the reissuing of out-of-print titles from its own backlist, producing digital reprints of books that are still sought after by scholars and students but could not be reprinted economically using traditional technology. The Cambridge Library Collection extends this activity to a wider range of books which are still of importance to researchers and professionals, either for the source material they contain, or as landmarks in the history of their academic discipline.

Drawing from the world-renowned collections in the Cambridge University Library and other partner libraries, and guided by the advice of experts in each subject area, Cambridge University Press is using state-of-the-art scanning machines in its own Printing House to capture the content of each book selected for inclusion. The files are processed to give a consistently clear, crisp image, and the books finished to the high quality standard for which the Press is recognised around the world. The latest print-on-demand technology ensures that the books will remain available indefinitely, and that orders for single or multiple copies can quickly be supplied.

The Cambridge Library Collection brings back to life books of enduring scholarly value (including out-of-copyright works originally issued by other publishers) across a wide range of disciplines in the humanities and social sciences and in science and technology.

Baroness
Burdett-Coutts

A Sketch of Her Public Life and Work

ANONYMOUS

CAMBRIDGE UNIVERSITY PRESS

Cambridge, New York, Melbourne, Madrid, Cape Town,
Singapore, São Paolo, Delhi, Mexico City

Published in the United States of America by Cambridge University Press, New York

www.cambridge.org
Information on this title: www.cambridge.org/9781108057226

© in this compilation Cambridge University Press 2013

This edition first published 1893
This digitally printed version 2013

ISBN 978-1-108-05722-6 Paperback

THE BARONESS BURDETT-COUTTS

BARONESS BURDETT - COUTTS
A SKETCH OF HER PUBLIC LIFE AND WORK PREPARED FOR THE LADY MANAGERS OF THE WORLD'S COLUMBIAN EXPOSITION BY COMMAND OF

HER ROYAL HIGHNESS, PRINCESS
MARY ADELAIDE, DUCHESS OF TECK

LONDON
UNWIN BROTHERS
27, PILGRIM STREET, E.C.
CHICAGO
A. C. McCLURG AND COMPANY
1893

CONTENTS.

CHICAGO, JANUARY, 1893

To Her Royal Highness,
    Princess Mary Adelaide,
        Duchess of Teck.

Madam,—I hope you will permit me as President of the Board of Lady Managers of the Columbian Exhibition to address Your Royal Highness on a matter of some importance, and one in which we venture to ask your gracious assistance.

Your Royal Highness will be aware that the Exhibition will include as one of its most valued features a Section devoted to the Philanthropic Work of British Women. This has been prepared by the Baroness Burdett-Coutts, the President of the Committee appointed for the purpose, and will, I understand, supply a most interesting

record of women's philanthropic work
in Great Britain. The fact, however,
that the Baroness has undertaken this
work, while greatly enhancing its importance and interest, gives rise to a
difficulty which will seriously impair
the value of the exhibit.   It is obvious
that no record of the Philanthropic
Work of Englishwomen could be complete, or in any sense satisfactory,
without some account of the great part
which the Baroness herself has taken
in such work.   Her name is almost as
well known and honored throughout
this country as it is in England, not
only for a long life of noble deeds, but
for the practical insight, untiring devo-
tion, and great wisdom, which she has
brought to bear upon philanthropic
subjects.

In reply to an official inquiry the
Baroness has informed me that as

President of her Section she does not propose to include any account of her individual work.

My Board considers it essential to the success of the exhibit that this deficiency should be supplied, and knowing that the Baroness has long enjoyed Your Royal Highness' friendship, extending to personal assistance in some of her works, we venture to turn to Your Royal Highness as one to help us to fill up the gap which I have indicated.

That object would be attained if Your Royal Highness could arrange that some record of the Baroness Bur⸱dett-Coutts' work could be supplied to the Exhibition, together, possibly, with any models or illustrations that may be available. For this purpose we should be happy to place a special position in the Women's Building at Your Royal Highness' disposal.

I need hardly add that by acceding to this request Your Royal Highness would confer a distinguished favor on the Board of Managers, and that such participation in our labors would be accepted as a very gracious act by all American women.

I remain with much respect,

Your Royal Highness' faithful servant,

BERTHA HONORÉ PALMER,

PRESIDENT OF THE BOARD OF LADY MANAGERS.

To Mrs. Potter Palmer,
PRESIDENT OF THE BOARD
OF LADY MANAGERS,
WORLD'S COLUMBIAN EXHIBITION.

MADAM,—I have much pleasure in
acceding to the request of the Board
of Lady Managers by presenting this
short record of the Baroness Burdett-
Coutts' philanthropic work to the Chicago Exhibition; for I fully appreciate
the inadequacy of any representation of
the Philanthropic work of British Women, which does not include the part
taken in it by the subject of this
record.

It is only just, I would not say to
English women, but to *all* women, that
one who has enriched the reputation of
her sex by her life, character and

deeds, should find a place in that department of your great Exhibition,
which is so wisely devoted to the
true public sphere of women's philanthropy.

I have known intimately the Baroness all my life, have valued her friendship, and have often participated in
some of her work, as did also my late
father, the Duke of Cambridge. The
Duke of Wellington, the Earl of Har-
rowby (the Baroness' cousin), and
others of their time, with whom I have
been acquainted, watched with interest
the earlier stages of a career which has
been so fruitful of benefit to her fel-
low-beings, and often assisted in her
undertakings. From that time down
to the present day the Baroness has
been prominent among the subjects of
the Queen in all good works. Your
letter shows so well that you appreciate

the real value of her work—its sagacity
and practical insight into the conditions of want and suffering, and their
effective amelioration—that I need not
say anything on this point.

I would like, however, to add two
remarks. Great as have been the in-
trinsic benefits that the Baroness has
conferred on others, the most signal of
all has been the power of example—an
incalculable quantity, which no record
of events can measure. She has ever
sought, also, to increase the usefulness
of women in their homes, to extend
their opportunities of self-improve-
ment, and to deepen the sources of influence which they derive from moral
worth and Christian life.

This record has been prepared at
somewhat short notice from such materials as could be readily found
under those circumstances, and by a

competent and accurate hand. It does not pretend to be complete or exhaustive, and the main object indicated to the compiler responsible for it, was to show in what varied spheres the Baroness' work has been placed, and by what kind of methods she has carried it out.

Sincerely congratulating you on your praiseworthy attempt to add still more to the renown of your wonderful Exhibition by thus giving prominence to the highest and best form of woman's work, and wishing you every success,

I remain,

Yours very faithfully,

MARY ADELAIDE,

PRINCESS OF GREAT BRITAIN AND IRELAND,

DUCHESS OF TECK.

INTRODUCTION.

The object of this little volume, prepared at the request of the Board of Lady Managers of the Chicago Exhibition, is to give a short general account of the public work of the Baroness Burdett-Coutts. Even within this limit, it does not pretend to be a complete record, and in no sense whatever is it a biography. It has been compiled, somewhat hastily, from sources which are generally accessible, and while the facts are accurately stated they must be taken as little more than typical and illustrative of the work of a long life "of golden days, fruitful of golden deeds," which cannot be enumerated in these pages.

The Baroness is the youngest daugh-

ter of Sir Francis Burdett, Bart., one
of the leading figures in the political
history of the early part of the century, and long the champion of popular
rights.   She is the grand - daughter of
the wealthy banker, Thomas Coutts,
whose immense fortune—at that day
perhaps unprecedented—was eventually bequeathed to her by his widow
This young English lady then found
herself at the head of one of the great
financial houses of the world, ranking
in London next only to the Bank of
England, while socially the unique
character of her position conferred
upon her informal privileges which
almost constituted a prerogative.   As
one of many ambitions, the gratification of which thus lay within the
grasp of the young heiress, a writer
declared that, with her wealth, she
might "purchase a principality."

But Miss Burdett-Coutts secured a nobler and wider rule. She enthroned herself in the hearts of the people and commanded the homage of those who represented all that was noblest and best in England. With a generous and ready sympathy she entered into the aspirations of the masses then struggling towards a better and happier life; while her character and position enabled her to direct aid and influence from many powerful sources into the same channel. None who fail to recognize this aspect of her life can in any way appreciate the Baroness' true position in the history of her time. She not only drew those around her into the circle of philanthropic work, but by means of an example, which women unknown to her in all parts of the world have recognized, she indirectly obtained vast and far reaching

2

results in the cause to which her life
has been devoted.

At her well known house in Stratton Street, London, she received sov-
ereigns, princes, ambassadors, states-
men, and world-famed commanders.
She was the friend of great scholars ;
and explorers, and missionaries came
to her from the farthest ends of the
earth. Young writers, actors and art-
ists, their fame then first bursting upon
the world, had already received from
her the earliest and sweetest words
of praise and encouragement. And
yet amid a life of such high and ab-
sorbing interest her mind was ever
silently working for the good of others, now on great schemes for the benefit of masses, now on some one of
innumerable little projects for the benefit of individuals. It is with the first
of these that this volume is specially

concerned. Her vast work of private and individual charity is one of which no living hand can ever write the history, and she herself would probably be the first to desire that it should remain unwritten.

THE

BARONESS BURDETT-COUTTS

I.

THE CHURCH OF ENGLAND.

The earliest efforts of Miss Burdett-
Coutts were devoted to the service of
the Church of England, which it was
her earnest wish to see firmly planted
in the Colonies. In the year 1847,
carrying this desire into effect, she endowed the Bishoprics of Capetown,
South Africa, and of Adelaide, South
Australia, both of them modeled exactly on the English system. About
ten years later she founded the Bishopric of British Columbia; providing
twenty-five thousand pounds for the
Endowment of the Church; fifteen
thousand pounds for the Bishopric;
and ten thousand pounds towards the
maintenance of the Clergy. In the

interval she had been engaged at home
in a munificent effort in the same cause.

In January 1846 a report was cur-
rent that Miss Burdett-Coutts had
signed a blank cheque, which she had
handed to the Bishop of London with
a request that he would fill it in for
such a sum as might be required to
build and endow "a handsome Church."
It was also said that this cheque had
been honored to the amount of thirty
thousand pounds. The report was not
exactly accurate; but as a matter of
fact Miss Burdett-Coutts did build a
Church, one of the most handsome
erected in London in modern times.
It was also true that a cheque for thirty thousand pounds proving altogether
insufficient, a further sum of about
sixty thousand pounds was provided
to carry this magnificent work to completion. On the 20th of July, 1847,
the first stone was laid of the Church
of St. Stephen, Westminster — erected
by Miss Burdett-Coutts to the mem-

ory of her father, Sir Francis Burdett, who for so many years had represented in Parliament the City of Westminster. The ceremony of consecration was performed on the 24th of June, 1850, the day being observed as a fête in Westminster, where some one thousand five hundred people, inhabitants, school children, and workmen, were publicly entertained. A few days afterwards a special visit was paid to the church and schools by the Prince Consort.

The church is the work of Mr. Ferry, the Manchester architect. It was the second church in London dedicated to St. Stephen, and it re-introduced the spire, which had then fallen into disfavor in London, as a feature in ecclesiastical architecture. The interior plan consists of a nave 79 feet long by 21 feet wide; North and South aisles of the same length, and 12 feet wide; and a chancel 43 feet in depth by 21 feet wide. The height from the

floor of the nave to the ridge of the
roof is 54 feet, that of the chancel 40
feet, and that of the side walls of the
aisles 20 feet. The tower at the North-
East angle of the nave opens into the
chancel by a deeply recessed and
moulded archway, within which stands
a fine organ. The chancel has a poly-
gonal ceiling, divided into panels, the
ribs being enriched by beautifully
carved and emblazoned bosses, and the
panels richly colored. The altar is
covered by a superb altar cloth presented by the Duke of Wellington.
The "Great Duke," whose warm friendship for the young heiress led him to
watch her opening career with deep
interest, also presented to the church
a silk curtain of the 16th century taken
from the tent of Tippoo Sahib at the
storming of Seringapatam. The nave
roof is of oak, and is divided by arched
trusses and interties, the arch princi-
pals resting upon stone capitals and
triple shafts, elaborately carved. The

aisle roofs are more enriched than the
main roof, but are similarly divided
by ornamental trusses and form arches
in their design, the spandrils being
filled with geometrical tracery. The
pulpit, over which is hung the silk curtain just mentioned, is of Caen stone ;
the plain base supporting a highly enriched corbelled front, while the sides
finish in spandrils, filled in with tracery-
work. The Church contains the tomb
of Dr. W. Brown, whose wife, Mrs.
Hannah Brown, the life long companion and dearest friend of the Baroness,
also rests under the Communion Table.

The building of the church involved
provision for the purchase of a site,
for the demolition of rows of poor
houses and compensation to the tenants, and also for a permanent and
liberal endowment fund. While St.
Stephen's was in course of construction,
Miss Burdett-Coutts provided a mission
church and schools in which a congregation was first collected From the

date of the consecration, she has borne
the cost of all repairs to the fabric,
salaries of all officials, and all extraordinary expenditure for religious and
educational purposes in connection
with the church. But St. Stephen's
is not, and obviously was never intended to be, only a church. Its
Foundress conceived and carried out
the idea of placing almost under the
shadow of the great Abbey, but in the
midst of a very poor district, a living
example of all the work and influence,
both spiritual and material, which can
be included in a great parochial organization. This work has been gradually
enlarged, and now includes Guilds for
men, boys, and girls; Communicants'
Guild for women: Missionary Lay-
helpers; Working and Friendly Societies; Social and Benefit Clubs of
various kinds; a Ringers' Guild; Tem-
perance Societies; Bible Classes; an
organization for District Visiting; and
a Soup Kitchen, from which nearly

seventy thousand dinners have been
supplied to the poor within the last few
years. The St. Stephen's Self Help
Club, a most interesting experiment
in co-operation, increased its operations
from seven hundred pounds to two-
thousand pounds a year within three
years, and is still maintaining its extraordinary progress. In connection with
the church were established the large
and eminently successful St. Stephen's
Schools, where fifteen thousand boys
and girls have been educated. These
Schools and a thriving Technical Institute which has grown out of them, are
more fully referred to in the chapter
which deals with the Baroness' work
in aid of education.

The first vicar of St. Stephen's,
Westminster, was the Rev. W. Tennant,
who died in 1879. He was succeeded
by Rev. W. M. Sinclair, who resigned
the living in 1889 on his appointment
to the Archdeaconry of London. His
successor was the present vicar, the

Rev. W. H. G. Twining, who for many
years had been connected with the
church as curate. The occasion of
his induction was seized upon by the
inhabitants of Westminster for a popular demonstration in honor of the
Foundress. The Baroness and Mr.
Burdett-Coutts were received at the
boundary of Westminster by the members of between thirty and forty Tem-
perance, Trade, and Friendly Societies,
who formed a long procession and
conducted the Baroness to the church,
through thronged and gaily decorated
streets. This demonstration, which
was of a very hearty and spontaneous
character, was gratefully acknowledged
by the Baroness.

In building, in the poorest district
of Carlisle, a second church dedicated
to St. Stephen, the Baroness supplied
a church to a previously existing congregation, which, under the care of the
Rev. A. Hodges, was at that time
meeting in what had formerly been a

warehouse for furniture. Even for this poor accommodation the people had been indebted to the liberality of the Dean, who, seeing this large and increasing population growing up with no place provided for public worship, had borne the expense of Mr. Hodges' work. These facts were mentioned to Miss Burdett-Coutts by the Bishop of Carlisle (Dr. Waldegrave) at the suggestion of Dr. Tait, then Bishop of Ripon, and afterwards Archbishop of Canterbury. "Did you ever ask Miss Burdett-Coutts to help you?" Dr. Tait said to his friend. "No," was the reply "nor do I think I have any right to do so, seeing that she is a perfect stranger to the diocese, and my acquaintance with her is but slight." But in the opinion of the Bishop of Ripon this was not a conclusive reply; he thought that Miss Burdett-Coutts "would be rather pleased than otherwise" at receiving such a request

The result of the appeal was that
Miss Burdett-Coutts erected a church;
a small sum, which had already been
raised towards this purpose through
the exertions of Mr. Hodges, forming
the nucleus of an endowment fund.
The church, which was designed by
Mr. James Nelson Jr., of Carlisle, is
110 feet in length and 60 feet
in breadth, with a tower and spire
reaching a height of 130 feet. It
contains seating accommodation for
six hundred people, including seats for
seventy children for whom a special
entrance is provided. The East and
West windows are fitted with beautiful
stained glass; there is a fine peal of
eight bells; and the late Archbishop of
Canterbury once described it as in
every way "a model church."

The foundation stone was laid by
Miss Burdett-Coutts in March, 1864,
when addresses were presented to her
by the Building and Endowment Committee, and by the inhabitants on the

parish. In acknowledging these the Foundress said, "The Bishop's Pastoral letter, which stated with unaffected and touching earnestness the need of his diocese, especially of this ancient border town, opened out to me an opportunity I was seeking, and seemed almost an answer to a thought in my mind." She added that when asked to lay the first stone of the church she "felt that a peculiar privilege was accorded to her. For beautiful and full of solemn meaning as such a ceremony must ever be, it becomes peculiarly so when it takes place under circumstances when the practical piety of the population has been tested through trouble and tribulation."

By May of the following year the building was completed, and the ceremony of consecration performed, Miss Burdett-Coutts expressing the hope "that a manly and virtuous ministry may preach and practice Christ's teachings within its walls to a faithful

and understanding people, and raise up
living souls to bear witness from generation to generation to God's revealed
truth, and the salvation of mankind."

A more intimate personal connection
with the village of Ramsbury, on her
father's Wiltshire estate, where she
spent the early years of her life, in-
duced the Baroness to purchase in
1872 the right of presentation to the
vicarage of Ramsbury, then in the gift
of the Lord Chancellor; the purchase
money, under the provisions of Lord
Westbury's Act, being funded for the
benefit of the incumbent. The church
of Ramsbury is famous in the ecclesiastical history of Wessex. It stands
upon the site of a much more ancient
building, and is itself of great antiquity,
none of the old walls now standing,
it is believed, being of later date than
the year 1220. Subterranean passages
still exist, which in early times afforded
communication with the palace of the

Bishop; and among the ancient monu-
ments are a tomb to the memory of
William de St. John, dating from about
the year 1325, and another, in the
North aisle, probably belonging to the
close of the Fifteenth century.

The church also contains the remains of the Baroness' father and
mother, Sir Francis and Lady Burdett,
whose funerals were the occasion of a
scene memorable in the annals of the
county. Sir Francis died in London
on the 23rd January, 1844, and while
his body was actually in course of removal to Ramsbury, Lady Burdett also
passed away. The first arrangements
were suspended in order to allow of a
double funeral. When a few days
later the hearse passed by, the roads
for very many miles from Ramsbury
were lined with the peasantry, who
stood bareheaded and with every man-
ifestation of sorrow for the loss of one
who had been for so many years the
idol of the people, and who was known
3

in his own counties of Wilts and Derby-
shire as a kind and generous landlord.
Nor was Lady Burdett less beloved by
the peasantry of the countryside than her
husband; and the memory of their kindness and interest in the welfare of all
those about them is still cherished and
spoken of in the two counties where the
large family estates are situated.

Interesting alike in its architecture,
history, and associations, the church
of Ramsbury had gradually fallen into
a deplorable condition, and in 1890 it
was found that without immediate restoration it was in danger of becoming
a ruin. These facts being reported to
the Patroness she offered a liberal do-
nation towards the expense of the
work, and also took immediate steps to
call a meeting at Marlborough, and in
other ways to awaken public interest
in the restoration. A sum of over
six thousand pounds was thus raised,
and the necessary repairs carried out,
under the direction of Mr. J. Arthur

Reeve, the well known architect of London. In addition to munificent donations to the restoration fund, the Baroness placed in the church a reading desk and choir stalls as a memorial to the Rev. H. Baber, the late vicar.

Shortly after purchasing the living of Ramsbury the Baroness also secured that of the adjoining parish of Baydon —a small village on the top of the Wiltshire Downs, some twelve miles from the nearest railway station.

As regards situation Baydon is one of the highest and most isolated villages in England. Formerly a chapel-of-ease to Ramsbury, the spiritual needs of the parish owing to the meager stipend and other causes had been much neglected when the Baroness become the Patroness of the living. Her first care was to repair the church and vicarage, and increase the value of the living in perpetuity by giving a considerable sum to Queen Anne's Bounty for the purpose.

On visiting the village shortly afterwards the Baroness found that many of the cottages of the agricultural laborers, who form nearly the whole of the population, were in a lamentable state of dilapidation. Instructions were at once issued to an agent to purchase these insanitary dwellings, and to replace them as speedily as possible by model cottages of the most improved type. A considerable amount of the best land in the parish was also acquired by the Baroness in order to provide the laborers with flower gardens, and allotments upon which to raise sufficient vegetables to supply each family all the year round. At the same time the Baroness had several tanks sunk in the chalk, from which the villagers could obtain an abundant supply of pure water, while formerly nearly all the water used had to be carried a long distance.

The parish, placed under the care of the Rev. Maurice Meyrick, soon came to be recognized as a model representative of the parochial system. During the past year her ladyship has again repaired the church, re-hung the bells, and placed a new roof on the nave, at a cost of nearly a thousand pounds.

This chapter may be closed with a mention of the fact that in addition to St. Stephen's, Westminster, three other Metropolitan churches have been built by the assistance of the Baroness, who placed in the hands of the Bishop of London a sum of fifteen thousand pounds to be applied at his discretion in church building. It is of course impossible to enumerate the munificent assistance which she has given throughout her life to the erection, restoration, and maintenance of churches. It is sufficient to say that few efforts of this kind have been launched without an endeavor on the part of those organizing them to obtain directly or indirectly the support of her coöperation.

II.

EDUCATION.

In the important field of education the Baroness by her personal influence and example has probably
achieved indirect results exceeding in
importance the immediate and practical work, extensive as that has been,
in which she has been personally engaged. But of her direct efforts for
the advancement of education, which
may be looked upon as the complement
of her work for the church, a few may
here be mentioned. She erected and
has entirely supported the handsome
schools attached to St. Stephen's, Westminster; she made an annual grant to
similar schools at Carlisle, Ramsbury,
and Baydon; she provided a site for
the schools of St. Anne, Highgate; and

she also found a third of the funds for
the erection of the schools of St.
Peter's, Stepney.

The schools of St. Stephen, Westminster, which naturally most closely
engage her attention, have always
taken the first rank, and have almost
invariably been found in advance of
the standards set by the Education
Authorities. Since their foundation
nearly fifteen thousand pupils have received instruction there; and a special
feature, which has long been noticed,
is that children in after years take the
places in the school formerly occupied
by their parents. The educational
work at Carlisle, towards which the
Baroness made an annual grant, was
first carried on in the old warehouse
already mentioned, which was soon so
crowded that two class rooms had to
be obtained in an adjoining cottage.
School buildings were annexed to the
church in 1867, and are still successfully conducted.

In 1865 Miss Burdett-Coutts gave to
the Rev. Edward Arnold, Inspector of
Schools for the Western District, the
details of a system (practically tested
by her in an agricultural district of
Devonshire) for providing schools for
small villages.   Mr. Arnold was so
impressed with the simplicity and
practical character of the scheme that
he communicated it to the Committee
of Council of Education, by whom it
was eventually adopted, and, though
omitted from a subsequent scheme of
Council, it still survives in Scotland.

This scheme was devised to meet
the needs of a very small country parish, where, owing to the small population, it was impossible to have a separate and well appointed school, and
the difficulties of a large and scattered
parish, where it would be impossible to
establish a school in any one spot that
would be reasonably accessible to all.
It provided for the re-establishment of
the cottage "dame-school " in each par-

ish, or in each sub-division of a large parish. These schools, which then existed in considerable numbers, were placed under the care of some person fit to discharge the humble duties required; and over a small group of schools was appointed a properly certificated master, who, treating these cottage-schools as being only class rooms of one large institution, attended each in succession for a day or two days at a time. On him rested all responsibility for the instruction of the children and for the organization of the schools, as well as for all other matters that usually constitute the duties of a master, and it was on the fact of his supervision that the demand for the Government grant was based.

Small fees were charged, and a capitation grant was made to the teachers, in addition to salary, for children passing the annual examination held by the Government Inspector in some central place convenient for the schools

of each group. Instruction was thus
placed within easy reach of all by the
simple expedient of bringing the
school to the children instead of re-
quiring the children to walk impossible distances to the school. As was
very aptly said at the time, "Each
group is a little University with half a
dozen affiliated colleges. The daily
routine of instruction is in the colleges,
with public lectures and examinations."

With an instinctive dread of education drifting into a system of mechanical instruction, the Baroness has always
taken a very broad view of the subject.
Her published addresses to the pupils
of the Whitelands Training College
show how clearly she saw the tenden-
cies of that day, and, still more, how
far she anticipated modern developments. As early as 1868 she deplored
the fact that "to pass or not to pass"
in certain set subjects was, with many
of the schools, the equivalent of "To
be or not to be." But her own ideal

was a much broader one. She called upon teachers to inculcate ideas of social duty; concisely adding that "to whatever class a person may belong, an industrious discharge of the duties of that position in life is a social and religious obligation." In a private letter, of about the same time, she shows her anxiety to impress upon all efforts to promote industrial training, "a feminine and domestic character." She speaks of the cultivation of habits of kindness to animals as "a fundamental part of education;" she refers to the refining influence of a love of flowers; and to the high educational importance of the preservation of "historic and patriotic associations;" and, above all, she insists on the personal influence of the teacher.

With these wide views, however, she by no means lost sight of practical detail. It was mainly through her efforts that the course of instruction in English schools was made to include such subjects as sewing and cookery. To the

latter she has devoted much time and
effort, and she has seen its importance
widely recognized in the National
Schools. But it must be remembered
that there was a time when the teaching
of cookery was unknown, and when the
suggestion of it would have been almost
laughed at. It was then by energetic
advocacy in London and the provinces,
that the Baroness convinced both the
people and the school authorities that a
far better and more effective use might
be made of the food at the command
even of the poorest by a sound knowledge of how properly to prepare it.

Systematic attempts were made by
the Baroness to diffuse a knowledge of
what are called "Common Things." At
Whitelands for many years she gave
prizes for papers on such subjects as
"Household Work," "Needle Work,"
"Country Matters," "Thrift," and
"Household Management." Speaking
on the subject treated in one of these

papers—"The Influence of the Head
of the Family"—Lady Burdett-Coutts
commented on a remark to the effect
that whom a woman appoints to that
position lies entirely within her own
choice. She added, "Teachers would
be doing a kindness to point out this to
their elder girls when they leave school,
and advise them, before they marry, to
observe carefully the habits, and conduct
towards others, of those who wish them
to enter into so serious and responsible
an engagement." She urged upon teachers the necessity of observing rules of
neatness and simplicity in dress, and
suggested, on one occasion, that by their
influence they might help to check an
unfortunate habit "which is widely
spread among us, of not seeming to
brush the hair any more, or of wearing
other people's," of which she indicated
the obvious dangers. These remarks
aroused a considerable amount of attention, though, lest it should be hastily
assumed that her comments were every-

where received with respectful defer-
ence, it should be mentioned that one
person at least raised a firm and formal
protest.   He wrote that with her "remarks regarding neatness, simplicity,
and decorum of appearance in dress, I
entirely concur. . . . With your Ladyship's remarks, however, regarding the
hair I cannot coincide."   He assumed
that the Baroness' knowledge was "only
theoretical," though "practical knowledge is the only way by which any one
can be an authority upon so important a
subject.   If the above remarks remain
uncontradicted they will be injurious to
the public," and he proceeded to explain
that his only object in writing was "to
allay the excitement which has taken
hold of the public mind since your
Ladyship's address was delivered"! In
this instance the Baroness' antagonist
turned out to be a hairdresser!

Among other educational efforts the
Baroness established an Art Students'

Home for ladies, the first of its kind
in London, though the need of it must
be obvious to any who bear in mind
the steady increase in the number of
ladies drawn to the Metropolis by the
facilities for study offered there by the
Museums and Institutions. This
Home has lately become self-support-
ing, and the chief importance attaching to it lies in its character as the
prototype of other and larger developments of the same idea in London.
In the work of the Birkbeck Literary
and Scientific Institute, of which her
father was one of the founders, Lady
Burdett-Coutts has shown much interest, and has twice presided at its in-
augural meetings. She was one of the
earliest champions of evening schools
for the poor. Hundreds of boys have
been educated at her expense on training ships, taken from the crowded
and destitute district of Spitalfields
and Bethnal Green, where dens of
thieves were broken up by her persist-

ent drawing away of their most promising recruits. These boys were afterwards fitted out for the Royal Navy
or the Merchant Service, and sometimes in other ways qualified for lives
of usefulness. For very many years she
maintained a large night school for boys
at Cooper's Gardens, in the East end of
London, and these premises she has
recently transformed into a gymnasium
and free reading room, the pressing
need of night classes having been supplied by the State.

An invitation to become a member
of the School Board for London was
addressed to the Baroness in 1870.
In declining this request her ladyship
expressed the opinion that she did not
think it advisable, under present circumstances, for women to hold such an
office, though she would be glad to see a
Sub-Committee of ladies appointed by
the Board, or by the Privy Council, for
the consideration of points connected
with the management of girls' schools.

The Baroness but recently organized a very complete educational
scheme in Westminster, by what was
practically an amalgamation and reconstruction of existing institutions, chief
among which were the Townshend Free
Schools, and the St. Stephen's Schools.

The former schools, first known as
the "Chauncey Hare Townshend Free
Schools," were the outcome of a bequest by the Rev. Chauncey Hare
Townshend. After munificent legacies
of pictures, gems, and scientific collections, to the National Museum at
South Kensington, this gentleman left
the whole of his personal property to
the Baroness Burdett-Coutts and the
Rev. Thomas Helmore, as trustees, to
found and endow a School, in or near
London, to provide education of "the
humblest and simplest kind" for the
very poor.

The testator wisely left the trustees
very considerable latitude as to the
method by which they would give ef-

4

fect to his intentions, and allowed them six years in which to come to a decision. Two years after Mr. Townshend's death, such simple education as he mentioned was publicly provided for the class he desired to benefit by the Education Acts of 1870.

Under these circumstances the original sum was allowed to accumulate for a time, occasional grants only being made in aid of training ships and other institutions of a similar kind, the bulk of the money being ultimately devoted in 1876, to the establishment of a free school in Rochester Street, Westminster, for children to whose parents the comparatively high fees then charged in Church and in Board Schools were a serious burden. Evening classes were also started for boys of thirteen years of age, in which respects the institution was the first of its kind in London.

By the passing into law of the Free Education Act of 1890 the rearrange-

ments of this Trust already referred to
were rendered desirable. Up to that
time the Townshend schools had provided practically free elementary education for the children of very poor
parents in widely separated districts of
London. Though a very considerable
number of the scholars were drawn
from Westminster and the adjoining
parishes, very many others were the
children of poor people living in nearly
all parts of the Metropolis. While the
State compelled parents to send their
children to an efficient elementary
school, the only provision made to relieve the extremely poor of the burden of the weekly school-pence was
one repugnant to the feelings of inde-
pendence of a respectable laborer.
Thus the children of many of the most
deserving poor of London flocked to the
Townshend Schools, where they either
received free education, or if their parents could afford to pay were asked
to contribute a penny per week to the

school funds.   From 1876 till 1891
some twelve hundred children were
yearly educated in these schools, which
generally earned the maximum Government grant, and both as regards teaching and discipline have repeatedly been
specially commended by Her Majesty's
Inspectors of Schools.

But the Education Act of 1890 entirely changed the existing condition
of things. Under its provisions schools
in every parish throughout the country
were either rendered entirely free, or
the fees reduced to a minimum.   The
Baroness Burdett-Coutts, therefore, felt
that it was no longer necessary or desirable to devote the funds of the
Townshend Trust to the maintenance of
a very large free school in Westminster, when nearly half the children attending it could obtain equally good
education in the new free schools near
their homes.   Owing to the popularity
of the Townshend Schools, and a pro
vision in one of the Education Acts

forbidding the managers of a school to
refuse admission to any child as long
as a vacancy exists in the accommodation, it was necessary to transfer the
teachers and scholars of the free
school to a smaller building. They were
accordingly placed in a portion of the
buildings until then occupied by the St.
Stephen's Church schools, and the
teachers and children in those over-
crowded and ever increasing schools
were transferred to the Townshend
buildings in the adjoining street. At the
same time the schools were renamed the
St. Stephen's Higher Grade Schools, and
the St. Stephen's Elementary Schools
(Townshend Foundation). The Elementary School was made entirely a
free school; while in the Higher Grade
School, in which extra subjects, such as
French, Latin, Mathematics, Geometry,
etc., are taught, a scale of moderate
fees ranging from two to six pence a
week is still maintained. A number of
free scholarships enable deserving

boys and girls to pass from the Elementary School through the Higher Grade School.

To complete this scheme of re-organization the St. Stephen's Technical Institute, long maintained by the Baroness, was much enlarged in its scope, and renamed the Westminster Technical Institute. To provide for its growing needs her ladyship has munificently supplied funds for the erection of a large building, which will contain excellent workshops, equipped with all necessary tools and appliances, and a technical library, etc., for the use of the students. When completed the Institute will probably be one of the finest of its kind in London.

The instruction given in the Westminster Technical Institute includes such subjects as Technical and Mechanical Drawing, Drawing and Shading from the Cast, Applied Art, Building Construction, Builders' Quantities, Carpentry and Joinery, Bricklayers

and Plumbers' Work, Metal Plate Work,
Cookery and Dressmaking, each subject
being taken by a teacher practically
engaged in the particular trade. Commercial and Civil Service classes,
classes in Shorthand, Bookkeeping,
Mathematics, French, German, and
other useful subjects, are also held,
and lectures are delivered on various
subjects of practical interest.

A feature calling for special remark
is that fifty scholarships have been
founded in the Institute by the Baroness as the Townshend Trustee, all of
which are for the benefit of poor or
deserving pupils attending the St. Stephen's Elementary and High Grade
Schools. These enable the children to
whom the scholarships are awarded to
attend the Institute free while they
remain in, and also after leaving the
day schools, and to receive the best
instruction in technical, art, scientific,
or commercial subjects. There are
also a large number of free scholar-

ships which are awarded yearly to the most deserving boys or girls of poor parents, recommended to the managers of the Institute, and a limited number of scholarships awarded by competitive examination.

The success of the Technical Institute, and the practical value of the work it is accomplishing, are shown by the fact that in 1892 out of four medals offered for competition throughout the country by the City and Guilds of London Institute for metal plate work, two were carried off by students of the Baroness' Institute, while many other distinctions were won by pupils in the examinations held under the Science and Art Department, South Kensington, the Education Department, and the Society of Arts.

To science and scholarship the Baroness has, directly and indirectly, rendered valuable support. The Burdett-Coutts Geological Scholarship, founded

by her ladyship, is one of the highest
scientific honors to be gained at the
University of Oxford. She did much
to help forward the work of the late
Sir Richard Owen, Sir Joseph Hooker,
Frank Buckland, and Professor Tennant ; and from her many other men
eminent in science, literature, and art,
have received encouragement and recognition long before their names were
known to the world. In the researches
of scholars and antiquarians into all
questions bearing upon the elucidation
and verification of the Scriptures, the
Baroness has always taken a deep
interest. She employed agents in the
East to secure old Biblical manu-
scripts, of which a large and very
important collection was formed. Of
these some have been presented by
the Baroness to public institutions ;
while the large number that remain in
her possession were placed at the use
of the late Dr. Scrivener, a member of
the Committees of the Revised Ver-

sions of the Old and New Testaments, and led to many new readings of obscure and difficult passages in the Scriptures.

A letter sent in 1880 by the Baroness, in reply to an address presented to her by the Vicar, Churchwardens and Vestry of St. Pancras, was ordered to be engrossed, framed, and hung in the Vestry Hall. It was a letter pleading for the preservation as public gardens of the old church yards, and is mentioned here because the Baroness' remarks afford an instance of how, unwilling to confine real education to a mere school routine, she has constantly pointed out the lessons which can be drawn from other sources. "The church yards and burying grounds," she says, "have brought down to us the memory of our forefathers, who have fought many a good loyal fight for many of our most valued national privileges, and as the names may only record sorrows, joys, and virtues, with which we are unconnected, history may suggest varied ways in which we may be still reaping the benefits of good local citizenship in past generations. It is certain that many pious, humanizing feelings, and much of the interest attaching to historic and patriotic associations, would be lost if the graves of the dead were obliterated from the land. The mere fact of closing over and stamping out of remembrance the dead, renders them lifeless indeed, and denies to their memory those tender and salutary lessons so often given in the quiet of God's acre."

III.

THE CRY OF THE CHILDREN.

To enumerate the various ways in which the Baroness has advanced the interests of the young would exceed the limits of this work. She has long been regarded as the friend of childhood, the cause of which she has pleaded during the whole of her long life by speech and pen, and still more often has forwarded by personal efforts, by appeals, and by wise counsel to various authorities. She takes an active interest in a host of institutions established for the benefit of children, and the protection of children against cruelty has been one of her most important works, carried on in conjunction with many influential persons whom she gradually attracted to the cause. Her attention

was early drawn to the pitiable plight
of children who come under the control
of their parents after those parents had
been found guilty of cruelty towards
them ; and nearly thirty years ago she
took up a resolute attitude with regard
to the treatment of children by the
poor law authorities.

In April, 1866, her attention was
keenly roused by a sad case of neglect,
and the sufferings of a child named
Green, who ultimately died in the infirmary of the St. Pancras Workhouse.
The child had been deserted in the
previous September. A letter request-
ing the authorities to remove it had
been sent by the father, who stated he
had left it in a room " without doors or
windows, and without food or help."
The child when taken to the workhouse
was in a debilitated condition, and
ultimately was seen to be dying.
Medical assistance was not obtained,
and a Scripture reader deposed that
the child was " laid out " for burial

while still breathing and moving. At
the inquest a severe censure was passed
on the superintendent, and the Scripture reader warmly commended.   But
the Guardians, strongly resenting the
denial of their right to do as they
pleased with their own poor, reinstated
the superintendent, and forbade the
missionary entrance to the workhouse.

This behavior aroused the deepest
indignation of the Baroness, whose
feelings will be best measured by the
letter she addressed to the Guardians.
After referring to the difficulties of
their position, between the payers of
rates on the one hand, and the
recipients of parochial relief on the
other, she said: "It appears to me
you have endeavored to favor the
former class by attempts to keep down
assessments at a cruel sacrifice of the
necessaries, sometimes of the lives, of
the paupers ; a kind of economy which
proves in the end a most expensive
economy ; for, putting aside all con-

siderations of Christian duty and
kindly feeling, a sick pauper is a costly
burden on the rates, and a more liberal
workhouse management would prevent
the crowding of infirmary wards. * * *
No excuse can be found in this circum-
stance for the mismanagement of the
sick wards of this workhouse. The
evidence given at the inquest on a
child prematurely laid out for dead
proved, indeed, that for the two-
thousand inmates of the workhouse,
the paid officials are far too few, and
it also proved from their own evidence
of their own proceedings respecting
the child in question, that these officials
are not fitted for the duties for which
they are paid." * * * Whatever the
state of the workhouse "the poor
child's fate ought to have excited
sorrow and sympathy, but the conduct
of the officials as reported in the newspapers, seems chiefly to have been
marked by an absence of any sense
whatever that the occurrence was one

at all calculated to shock the commonly
decent and humane.   Such a hideous
instance of callousness makes those
shudder who feel they are forced by
law to pay a rate which places the sick
in similar hands.

"As a rate-payer I feel the position
in which I am placed very keenly.
The law compels me to pay a rate for
the benefit of the poor, but in its
administration the law not merely fails
to secure the object of the rate, but
exposes the recipient of parochial
relief, according to the evidence before
the Coroner, to being 'laid out' before
death whenever the nurses, matron or
lady-superintendent, or whatever the
designation of the responsible persons
may be, may choose to think the victim
of their neglect cannot 'last long,' or
is 'nearly gone.'"

In 1883 the Baroness wrote to the
Home Secretary calling his attention
to the work of "a small society" for
the defense and protection of children,

especially dwelling on "the frequency
and varied forms of child abuse and
cruelty as reported in the daily papers,
and, secondly, on a grave defect in the
present state of the law—namely,
that after conviction and punishment
of offenses against the person in the
case of children there is no subsequent
protection whatever to those children;
they remain again in the custody and
absolute power of those who have already injured them." She called attention to the injury the country sus-
tained by the loss of these children
"consigned to death by their unnatural
parents as lightly as they were brought
into life," and gave point to her rep-
resentations as to the defenselessness
of the children by mentioning recently reported cases of a scandalous
character.

The "small society" here mentioned
developed rapidly, and is now known
as the National Society for the Prevention of Cruelty to Children, of which
5

the Baroness is a trustee. This Society is now dealing annually with
nearly ten thousand cases of wilful
neglect of, or cruelty to, children.
But it is not a mere prosecuting Society. It holds that proceedings in
Court are neither wise nor good when
the proper treatment of children can
be attained by any other means, and
it is found that in the majority of
cases a warning orally delivered or a
formal printed notice is sufficient to
stop the evil.

Under the auspices of this Society a
Bill for the protection of Children was
prepared in 1888, public attention being called to the proposed measure in
a letter written by the Baroness to the
press in October of that year. A
shocking case of ill-treatment by a
drunken mother had come before the
police courts; it was proved that the
woman had made her child, a girl of
ten, lie in a bed in which was the body
of her dead father. The case gave a

horrible significance to the Baroness'
repetition of the fact that the mother
on her release would be legally entitled to the custody of that child. In
1889 the Bill passed into law. This
Act, which is now often spoken of as
"the Children's Charter," made fundamental changes in the standing of
English children. It gave them a
legal right to clothing, food, and
proper treatment; threw the Courts of
Law open to them, and admitted as
legal evidence the testimony of an innocent parent, whose mouth had formerly been sealed. Above all, in such
special cases as that just mentioned,
it authorized the removal of children
from the custody of parents, and placing them in the care of guardians appointed by the Court, and the compul-
sion of parents deprived of the custody of
their children to contribute towards
their support. This alteration of the
law was specially needed in order to
ensure the detection and punishment

of offenses against children when committed, as is unfortunately somewhat frequently the case, by persons in comparatively high positions. The Society is now engaged in promoting legislation on the evils of baby-farming and child life-insurance.

The Baroness succeeded the Earl of Shaftesbury as President of the Destitute Children's Dinner Society, the merciful work of which has been quietly and most successfully conducted for nearly thirty years. The object of this society is to give supplementary assistance to the dining rooms opened for children, who for a penny or half-penny can there procure a substantial and nutritious meal. It is calculated that every additional sovereign given provides a dinner for one hundred children; and a shilling provides a dinner for four. The dinner consists of Irish stew with a fixed quantity of meat, vegetables and rice.

These dining rooms, about sixty in number, are partly supported by the pence and halfpence of children attending the Board or Voluntary Schools — payment of the small contribution being enforced as strictly as charitable feeling will allow. Some three hundred thousand dinners are given each season. The Baroness has been successful in arousing the interest of more happily situated children by whom dinners are as regularly seen as the sun, in the welfare of their "less fortunate comrades, living in lands where regular dinners are unknown."

IV.

PROTECTION OF ANIMALS.

The formation of habits of kindness
to animals, which seems the complement of her work on behalf of children,
is, in the opinion of the Baroness, "a
fundamental part of education;" her
own innate love of animals of all kinds
finding expression in another of her own
phrases, "Life, whether in man or beast,
is sacred." Fond of horses, and a prac-
ticed rider in her earlier days, she was
the constant companion of her father,
Sir Francis Burdett, who was one of the
most accomplished horsemen of his
time. She has maintained this interest in
the noblest of animals up to the present
day, and has kept, and still keeps, pets
of every kind. A bird of preternatural
gravity, the Stratton Street parrot, wel-

comes the coming or speeds the parting
guest with an aptness and fluency of
expression invariably startling; and a
more showy, if less gifted, comrade finds
infinite solace in the monotonous repetition of his own name. For years the
Baroness kept llamas in her grounds
at Holly Lodge, where a white donkey,
brought to her by costermongers, now
leads a life of pampered indolence. Her
dogs are almost public characters in
London. She has always kept a herd
of cows of a special breed; but, as in
other departments of her work, her
active attention has been mainly devoted to the humbler animals, the encouragement and protection of which
was largely neglected. Her efforts on
behalf of bee-culture extended that
useful but lowly industry, by means of
the Society of which she is President,
amongst the peasantry of every county
in England, while the advantages afforded by the goat, "the poor man's
cow," have been constantly urged by

means of the British Goat Society, of
which she is also the President. Her own
goats are famous at all British Shows.
And, though the "leading" brief must
always be allowed to Charles Lamb,
yet there can be no doubt that prece-
dence must next be accorded to the
Baroness after her friendly apology,
made to an Irish journalist, for "the
companionable and reproductive pig,"
which, with other live stock in Ireland,
"rambles in and out of the poor hovels
with an easy familiarity displeasing,
probably, to the Sanitary Inspector,
but not altogether unattractive to
the eyes of a member of the Society
for the Prevention of Cruelty to
Animals !" In a word, to every effort
made to prevent suffering to the dumb
creation, whether by ensuring the punishment of wanton cruelty, or by speaking to the conscience of others guilty
only of the cruelty involved by want of
thought, or by investigations having for
their end the minimizing of evils that

cannot be entirely removed—to all these things her ladyship has ever accorded her most ready and eager assistance.

A characteristic letter appeared in 1871, giving an instance of the cruel worrying of stray or homeless dogs in the London streets. "A friend of mine brought to my stables last Sunday evening a small retriever puppy, hopelessly injured, and, after some attempts on the part of my coachman to heal and help it, there was evidently in mercy but one course to pursue, and the little creature can now never be hurt again. Should those who hounded it about Piccadilly that Sunday afternoon chance to read this narrative, it may gratify them to learn that their endeavors to deprive an unoffending animal of life succeeded. Perhaps, also, at some odd moment of their own lives they may not be sorry to know that it did not pant out its dying minutes in the cold, misery, and fear, in which a brave woman saw,

pitied, and protected it. Whoever that
lady may have been, she must certainly
be a comforting person to have near
one in any moment of doubt and difficulty; for it required some nerve, as
well as a tender heart, to stand up, as she
did at the corner of Berkeley Street,
attracting a motley crowd around her,
yet unwilling to leave the trembling
animal to whom a kindly instinct had
brought her, until my friend, who was
accidentally passing at the moment,
came to the rescue. I tell the story as
it happened in the hope that it may
illustrate the necessity of a systematic
teaching of the duty of the humane
treatment of animals. While all that
relates to animal life affects indirectly
the welfare and safety of man — and the
close connection should never be lost
sight of — yet, even apart from and be-
yond all this, the inhuman treatment of
animals should be held to be a wrong
and a sin. Until the law, the main edu-
cator of the people, fully recognizes

this principle, the evil will never be fully remedied. The law itself, however, is also a reflex of the education of the people, and it is in education, therefore, that a remedy for this prevalent vice must ultimately be found."

In 1872 the Baroness also wrote to *The Times* calling attention to the cruel trapping of singing birds, and stating that she had been selected by the Ladies Committee of the Royal Society for the Prevention of Cruelty to Animals, "to represent the pitiable case of our little clients." She complains in her letter that she has made several successful efforts to induce the nightingale to build in the gardens of her house at Highgate, but ultimately all were snared. "Not caring to breed nightingales for bird fanciers" she has had to give up the attempt, but enters a strong protest against the demoralizing practices of bird catchers. "I allude to the taking away from the creature God's gift of sight by the application

of acids or a red hot iron in order to
qualify it to act more efficiently as a
decoy to its unsnared companions. I
also refer to the scarcely, if at all, less
cruel practice at the bird mart of training by means of perpetual darkness, as
well as enveloping tiny cages in thick
coverings so that the poor blinded
occupants, surrounded by cages of
non-singing birds, uncovered and for
sale, may attract a multitude of dupes
by their superior music, which these
persons imagine issues from the throats
of the timid little creatures they purchase and carry to their homes." A
pitiful remonstrance was also raised
against the cruelty so caused to the
neglected progeny in the breeding season for which the Baroness demanded
a remedy. "Life is in itself too sacred
for those who inherit it to be tor-
tured or tormented with impunity, and
the habitual and unchecked license in
regard to the destruction of animal
life must react most injuriously on

man. * * * Might it not be wise to
impose additional checks, and to impress on the cruel, the thoughtless and
the heartless, through the law, that
life, whether in man or beast is sacred
in its eye, and that animals endowed
with sensation are given to man for
use, and may not be lightly regarded by
him, and must never be abused.''

An Act giving this protection was
introduced into Parliament and passed
into law; but the Baroness is still
found quietly, but persistently, taking
every opportunity of calling attention
to the subject, as she did, for example,
at a Christmas dinner given in Spitalfields early in January, 1873, when she
requested every one present, to assist
in disseminating the regulations laid
down in the measure; an abstract of
which, as well as of other measures of
interest to the working classes, she
directed to be prepared for their guidance.

About this time the facts of the life

of "Grey Friar's Bobby" were brought
before the Baroness.   This name refers
to a little dog, belonging to a man
named Grey, who on his death in 1858
was buried in the Grey Friar's Churchyard in Edinburgh.   At the burial his
faithful dog was the most conspicuous
mourner.   The following day the little
creature had been found lying on the
grave, and in accordance with the
rules, had been chased out of the
Churchyard.   But he was found there
again both on the second and the third
morning shivering in the wet and cold,
when the old caretaker, James Brown,
took pity upon and fed him.   The
grave was soon leveled by time.   It
had never been distinguished by
any mark or stone; but the dog
continued to visit the spot regularly—so regularly that he became well
known in the neighborhood and was
daily fed by one or two of the resi-
dents, and though many efforts were
made to entice him away none were

successful. On the imposition of the dog tax many persons wrote asking permission to pay for "Bobby." The Lord Provost of Edinburgh, however, exempted him, and presented the dog with a handsome collar, studded with brass nails, on which was the inscription "Grey Friar's Bobby, presented to him by the Lord Provost of Edinburgh, 1867."

It was to the memory of this faithful creature that the Baroness erected a handsome fountain at the corner of George IV. bridge. The structure is seven feet in height, and of beautiful red granite. The base affords a drinking place for dogs ; above it, supported on a cylindrical column, being the principal basin with a diameter of nearly four feet, and modeled after a classic vase. A second column rising from this supports a bronze sitting figure of "Bobby," the story of whose life is given on a bronze plate let into the monument. This inscription in

English, and rendered into Greek (by
the learned and large-hearted Professor Blackie), reads as follows:

THIS MONUMENT WAS ERECTED
BY A NOBLE LADY,
THE BARONESS BURDETT - COUTTS,
TO THE MEMORY OF
GREY FRIAR'S BOBBY,
A FAITHFUL AND AFFECTIONATE
LITTLE DOG
WHO FOLLOWED THE REMAINS OF
HIS BELOVED MASTER
TO THE CHURCHYARD
IN THE YEAR 1858,
AND BECAME A CONSTANT VISITOR
TO THE GRAVE,
REFUSING TO BE SEPARATED
FROM THE SPOT
UNTIL HE DIED
IN THE YEAR 1872.

After a visit to Edinburgh, the Baroness addressed a letter to the Scottish
Society for the Prevention of Cruelty to
Animals, on the subject of an application
to Parliament by the Tramway Companies praying to be released from an
obligation to extend their line. In the
course of the letter her ladyship spoke
very strongly on the condition of the
horses used on the Edinburgh tramway.

"Those who compel these miserable skeletons to toil and sweat up the incline of Leithwath and the North Bridge are surely daily committing breaches of the Act of Legislature both for prevention of cruelty to animals, and for the suppression of habits tending to the demoralization of the public. * * * I venture most earnestly to set before you this flagrant violation of these Acts. I feel that those who habitually see these horses so maltreated cannot exonerate themselves from great blame if they permit, without protest, this open violation of the right of every creature to good and fair treatment from the hands of man. * * * The misery from fear and suffering to the wretched horses must be very great ; the dread of falling must nearly equal the anguish of the renewed exertion to get up the cruel incline at any cost. The ingenuity of cruelty soon learns to inflict the stimulus of pain so useful when

6

physical power fails, in order to accomplish the task horses and drivers have to perform. It is impossible to express what I feel on seeing these animals, all my life accustomed to horses as I have been. Knowing that a horse would rather die than not do its work, I can estimate what the animal endures when it needs to be goaded to the task it has to perform."

The Baroness has raised her protest against the use of humming - birds, wings, or feathers, in ladies' dress, which she has characterized as "a mode of ornamentation which must suggest a blood stain on the delicate hat or cap."

She called public attention to the cruelties of the over - sea cattle trade, and also experimented with a new cattle truck in which some animals were sent from Edinburgh to London, and arrived, eating and drinking on the way, in a condition very different to that in which they usually came. Experi-

ments were made at her expense in
transforming the old trucks and fitting
them with the later improvements.
She posted in her market copies of the
Acts of Parliament for the punishment
of cruelty to animals, and for the use
of blasphemous language. In another
chapter will be found some reference
to the Baroness' interest in the poor
and deserving class of retail traders
known as costermongers, and it is only
necessary to state here that her sympathy was extended to the donkeys
and ponies which render such good
service to these peripatetic traders.
She built extensive and healthy stables
for them on the Columbia estate, in
East London, and also instituted donkey shows there, awarding prizes to the
costermongers who could bring forward animals in the best health and
condition, and prove them to have
been their property for at least six
months. In recognition of this work
she was presented by the Columbia

Costermongers' Club with an address
and a silver model of a donkey.
During the ceremony of presentation
a living specimen was introduced and
exhibited on the platform by its owner,
who had completely cured it of a broken leg, by careful attention.

Recently encouragement of a very
practical character has been given to
this cause in London by the establishment of the Cart Horse Parade Society,
in which the Baroness has taken an active interest. The drivers of vans and
wagons are encouraged to bring together in friendly competition the
animals and vehicles in their charge,
usually on the Whit-Monday Bank
Holiday—and prizes are awarded by
the Society to the man whose horses,
harness, and turn-out give evidence of
kind and careful attention. Additional
prizes are also given by the Shire
Horse Society for the best animals in
make and shape. There is always an
enormous crowd gathered to see the

procession of three hundred carts, wagons and trolleys, many of which are drawn by teams of two, three, and four horses each. The number of competitors increases every year, and the operations of the Society, which was only founded in 1886, have been attended with a most gratifying success, justifying the theory of its founders, that more can be done to ensure good treatment of these animals by rewarding their attendants for good care than by prosecuting them for isolated cases of cruelty and neglect.

The work though so recently established in London had been known some years earlier in the provinces. On May - Day, 1882, the Baroness attended a parade at Newcastle, and, in the language of the local paper, "a hundred thousand people came into the town that day to see the Baroness." Besides cart and wagon horses the men from the collieries brought the pit-ponies, with the diminutive trolleys

drawn by them underground.   In the
report of the meeting a characteristic
incident is mentioned.   A request had
been made that the spectators would
not cheer the awards owing to the ex-
citable nature of some of the horses.
"The audience appeared to be quite
willing to follow the rule laid down, for
there was comparative quietness when
a horse took the first prize in Class I,
for teams of not less than four horses;
but the silence was broken by loud
and enthusiastic cheers when the.
driver, taking off his cap, seized hold
of the Baroness' hand and shook it
heartily.   Afterwards as each recipient
of a prize came forward the Baroness
greeted them in a similar fashion."
The Baroness declared that the remembrance of her reception that day would
long remain in her memory, with that
of "the long procession of splendid
horses, smaller but no less handsome pit-ponies, and humbler but no
less appreciated donkeys," and loud

cheers, and a cry of "God bless you," were evoked by her concluding remark that, "in this life man and beast are held together by God's own chain under one law."

The Baroness' work in connection with the Royal Society for the Prevention of Cruelty to Animals is too well-known to need much comment. She has long been President of the Ladies' Committee of the Society, the section upon which a large amount of important work falls, and her position has been very far from a merely titular one for she has regularly taken part in the work of the Committee, and has spoken at meetings in all parts of the country. As will appear only natural to those acquainted with her work on education, she has earnestly advocated and supported the educational work of the Society, which was initiated by her at the suggestion of Mr. Angell of Boston (Mass.), a gentleman who, abandoning a lucrative legal practice,

made the cause of dumb animals his
life's mission.   Immediately on his
visit to England he called upon the
Baroness, who, a few days later, expressed her determination to do all
she could "to form a Ladies' Humane
Society, the object of which should be
to inculcate in some definite manner
in all the schools of Great Britain
principles of humanity towards animals."   This work was undertaken by
the Ladies' Committee of the Royal
Society for the Prevention of Cruelty
to Animals already referred to, which
was formed very shortly afterwards, and
has effected an incalculable improvement in the tone of public feeling on
this subject.   Pupils in nearly every
school of the country contribute essays
on the "Treatment of Animals," for
the best of which prizes are awarded
or certificates conferred, the distribution having once been made by the
Queen in person, and frequently by
other members of the Royal Family.

V.

WORK AMONG THE POOR.

The work of the Baroness has always lain among the poor, generally
among the very poor, and a great part
of it has been connected with East
London. The following pages give
some indication of the character of this
work, though, as will be seen, no description is attempted of the large
amount of her private or individual benevolence which accompanied that
here mentioned. From about the year
1860, she practically supported the
East End Weavers' Aid Association, established for the relief of the hand-
loom weavers, whose occupation was
destroyed by the Treaty made with
France in 1860, on the basis of re-
ciprocity, under which large quantities

of French silks were imported. Some
of these weavers were started in small
shops, others were sent abroad as emigrants, and the young girls were trained
for service. But to provide for the
more helpless members of the class
Miss Burdett-Coutts opened an Institution in Brown's Lane, the work of
which was by no means of so re-
stricted a character as might be in-
ferred from the modest title of the
"Sewing School." And if the establishment is to be spoken of as a
"School," it must also be mentioned
that its pupils were not young. Young
girls were received only to be trained
for service; not to be taught so poor
a trade as that of the sempstress,
though it was often necessary to teach
them the use of the needle. Its purpose was to afford elderly women
recommended by want and good
character, the opportunity of spending
a profitable afternoon each day.

The school was opened at half past

one o'clock, and before beginning their duties each worker was provided with a good meal of soup and bread. The work given out was shirt making for the army and police forces, for which the women were paid at the rate of five-pence half-penny, for the hand stitching, the work having been previously cut out and the main parts roughly put together by the sewing machine. Work was also given to outside hands, properly recommended, who took away with them materials for six or twelve shirts, and were paid as they returned the finished shirts one or two at a time. Needles were sold at cost price, and cotton and other necessaries were provided gratuitously. The average sum earned by each was about eight shillings weekly, rising in individual cases as high as fifteen shilings; this very material addition to the scanty income of a family, earned in the intervals of domestic duties, representing exactly the difference between hard want and a comfortable living. About five hundred women were assisted in this manner in the course of the year, a third of the number being indoor hands.

Connected with the Sewing School was also a complete system of carefully devised help for the poor of the surrounding districts, of which one of the chief features was the visiting of the sick by professional nurses and the clergy. On their report, furnished each afternoon to the manager, there were distributed from the institution, meat, wine and other comforts, maternity boxes, and blankets. Young servants, going to a first situation were provided with a complete outfit in which to make a becoming appearance before their new employers. Similar outfits were also provided for lads going to sea, and casual work in the afterpart of the day was provided for the unemployed workman, who, while being free to seek permanent employment, was thus enabled to keep his humble home intact.

The extent of the work it is now very difficult to trace; but its complete and carefully organized character may be realized by a casual reference, in the press, to the work going on in August, 1867, at the time of the cholera epidemic in East London, when "Miss Burdett-Coutts distributed in one week one thousand eight hundred and fifty meat tickets of the value of a shilling each, 500 lbs. of rice, 250 lbs. arrow-root, 50 lbs. sago, 50 lbs. tapioca and oatmeal, 20 gals. beef tea, 30 lbs. black currant jelly, 80 quarts per day of pure milk supplied from her own farms, 400 yards of flannel, 200 garments and 100 blankets, 25 gallons of brandy, and 50 gallons of port wine." To the staff of three nurses regularly employed by her in the district she added five more, under the direction of a medical officer. She appointed two sanitary inspectors, and four distributors of the

disinfectants which she supplied. At
the same time vast quantities of bed-
ding were sold at cost price to the people, and many new appliances and
suggested remedies were practically
tested; while books and pamphlets,
containing valuable suggestions as to
the modes by which sanitary and
other improvements of a simple kind
might be effected in their homes
by the poor, were also widely distributed.

When in the bitter winter of 1861
the tanners of Bermondsey were un-
able to follow their occupation, Miss
Burdett-Coutts provided means of sav-
ing their homes. And on an intima-
tion by one of the Metropolitan Magistrates that money was less needed by
them than personal assistance in the
investigation of applications and the
distribution of the relief, she appointed
an agent to attend at the police courts
and when desired to afford such assistance.

Costermongers were assisted by the formation of a club with the object of advancing money to members for the purchase of barrows, the amount being repaid at the rate of a shilling per week, the sum usually charged by owners for the hire of such vehicles. The club has ever since been quite independent of eleemosynary aid, and its affairs are effectively conducted by its own members. Her ladyship's interest in the street vendor extended not only to the "coster's" business, but embraced his recreation. She sent a party of them to witness Mr. Irving's performance of "Hamlet." The men were carefully coached, reading and discussing the play with the manager at Brown's Lane, and thus were enabled to follow intelligently the performance of the great actor. Her interest in the class has continued up to the present time. During last year the whole of this street trade was seriously threatened in the law courts at the instance of local authorities. Summonses were taken out for a test case, and the whole practice of street or barrow dealing in London was in danger of being abruptly terminated. In this crisis the costermongers turned to their old protector, and the Baroness directed her own solicitor to take up their case with the aid of an able barrister. The case went against her clients in this first court, but the decision has since been reversed in the Court of Appeal, and the streets where the men habitually did their trade are still alive on Saturday nights with the barrows and stores, laden with every conceivable commodity, around which, under the flaming gas-jets, crowd the poorest of the London population.

The Baroness has followed with great sympathy the work initiated by Mr. Groom, who in 1886 organized some classes for the benefit of flower-sellers around Covent Garden Market.

In 1879 she formed the Flower-girls'
Brigade, enrolling as an organized
body, flower-sellers between the ages
of thirteen and fifteen. They were
appointed to special stations and placed
under protection of the police, while
efforts were made to secure for them a
permanent clientele. But having in
mind the undesirable character of such
an occupation for young girls, the
Baroness opened a factory where any
of the girls who desired to do so might
enter for one or two years, and receive
instruction in the art of artificial
flower-making. Others were trained
for domestic service and other work,
every endeavor being made to with-
draw the girls from their earlier calling.
Some eight hundred girls have been
trained in the factory, and the average
of failures is not over five per cent.

A somewhat similar work in which
the Baroness has had some interest,
though necessarily not an active interest, is that of the Charter Street Ragged

7

Schools in Manchester, one feature of which is a paying home for factory girls, who, failing the accommodation there provided, would have been compelled to seek shelter in the common lodging-houses.

In 1869 the Baroness issued an invitation to a conference at Columbia for the purpose of considering "how far it is possible to mark out the separate limits of the poor law and of charity respectively, and how far it is possible to secure joint action between the two." She also coöperated in 1879 with the East London Relief Committee, appointing almoners, for whose guidance sets of rules were prepared, and a scale of relief fixed.

The Baroness has established a number of other organizations in the same districts, including a Boys' Club designed to draw off from the street the crowd of lads who spend their evenings in drinking and gambling, a Shoeblack Brigade and Mission Church. At the same time her charity was never indiscriminate, and Sir Charles Trevelyan, speaking for one of the societies for the organization of charity, publicly admitted that "after careful examination" they found the principles on which they acted had been anticipated by her.

Mention may also be made of the Baroness' interest in flower-shows, especially in large towns, as an evidence of her recognition in "common things" of educational influences tending to the refinement of the minds and the daily life of the poor. One of the best known of these exhibitions is that in connection with the Lansdowne Place Ragged Schools, Tabard Street, Borough, London, where plants are given out early in the year to be returned for competition at the end of the summer in the best possible condition; the work has been so successful that parents have requested the committee to open the competitions to them as well as to the children.

Beneath "the lowest deep" there lies in the minds of the poor, a "lower deep," grimly represented by the union workhouses and kindred institutions, over which the Baroness has always exercised a careful vigilance. There is an occasional tendency to harsh and arbitrary exercise of authority by persons employed by public bodies to carry into effect, in a manner consistent with the spirit of humanity in which they were framed, the laws for the relief of the poor, and especially of the aged poor. At other times these duties are inefficiently performed. Against both evils her ladyship has always raised her protest. She insists on the essentially charitable nature of the payment—compulsory payment though it be—made by ratepayers in the form of poor rates, and has always been prompt to state the rights of the

beneficiaries when they appeared not
to be receiving the benefit to which
they are legally entitled.

Reference has already been made to
the case of the child in the infirmary
of St. Pancras, and to the careless performance of their duty by those in
charge, so strongly condemned by the
Baroness. In a letter written in 1887,
she is similarly seen endeavoring to
mitigate the hardship, in exceptional
cases, of regulations wisely framed to
meet general cases. The Baroness
recalls the facts elicited at an inquest
held to inquire into the cause of death
of an old man named Ansdells,
aged eighty-eight, who died of starva-
tion. The old man and his wife, who
had lived together for fifty-six years,
might have gone into the workhouse;
but to this they would not consent,
owing to a regulation by which they
understood that they would have been
separated the one from the other. At
the inquest it was pointed out that

under a special rule they might have
claimed exemption from the regulation;
but of this fact the old people were
evidently unaware, and certainly it is a
privilege very unusual in workhouses.
" Perhaps," her ladyship wrote, "it is
against all the principles of political
economy, and perhaps also it is morbid
and sentimental, to wish that such a boon
could be more generally conceded, or
that a slightly enlarged amount of
relief to three shillings and sixpence a
week could be allowed to aged couples
respectively past eighty and seventy,
who could not reasonably be expected
to be many years longer on the parish,
but who might have a wish to die in
each other's companionship."

After referring to a remark made by
a juror to the effect that the poor
generally shared the impression of the
Ansdells as to the workhouse rules,
which her ladyship confirms, she adds :
"I feel justified in saying that such
cases are rarely, if ever, found among

those applicants who appeal to that
lavish and indiscriminate charity said
to be so common among us. I hope
this special instance brought into
public notice through an inquest, may
awaken an interest in aged couples
situated as were Ann and Thomas
Ansdells, and feeling as they did, which
may lead to an amelioration of their
position." In conclusion the Baroness
called attention to the many encourage-
ments and aids to thrift now existing,
by means of which it is in the power
of all young men and women marrying
to-day, to secure to themselves a
shelter when age, sickness, and feeble-
ness, come upon them.

She was more than once nominated
to serve as Guardian of the Poor for
the Parish of Bethnal Green, and the
prospect of her election was received
with considerable gratification by the
press speaking in the name of the
poor, but the Baroness did not think it

advisable to assume the position, and requested the authorities to remove her name from the list of candidates. One reason, among others, for this step was a feeling that the fact of residing at such a distance from the locality interested would, in a sense, disqualify her for the duties of the office

VI.

COLUMBIA SQUARE.

THE gulf dividing the West from the East End of London, deep as it now is, was deeper twenty-five years ago It was a subject on which Charles Dickens often dwelt. He speaks of the journey from the one district to the other as one of the most extraordinary transitions that could be experienced. In one of his articles he has written of the wealth and luxury, flowers and perfumes, the rich houses and luxurious equipages of the wealthy district, asking : " Are care, illness, sorrow, death, known in such a place? Who are all these people and how are all these palaces maintained, where do the inhabitants, where does the money come from?" Then he turned suddenly east-

ward to a locality where, in his own
words, violence, cruelty, immodesty,
and uncleanliness, were unmitigated
and almost unconcealed. "Every
thing is perverted. Childhood is old
and careful. Infants, imitating the
violence they have seen about them
from their earliest recollection, are
shrill and shrewish with the smaller infants placed under their care. The
home is perverted from being a haven
of rest, which the man longs to get to,
and is become an earthly hell which he
has cause to dread. The women are
perverted to be unwomanly, and the
men, for the most part, to be like the
brute creation, with just enough humanity to make them more elaborate in
brutishness. The air is perverted to
carry from window to window the mon-
strous vapors encircled in a compound
interest of corruption as it passes on.
The sun's rays are perverted, and, instead of bringing wholesomeness and
purity with them, draw up a new wealth

of nastiness from every nook and corner, and, heating it to fever pitch, breed
death far and near."

In the center of this district, which
Miss Burdett-Coutts visited with Dickens, was a spot known as Nova Scotia
Gardens. There was a fine irony lurk-
ing in the poetic designation, for it
was here that every evil of the neighborhood existed in an exaggerated
form. There was a large piece of
waste ground covered in places with
foul, slimy looking pools, amid which
crowds of half-naked, barefooted,
ragged children chased one another.
From the center rose a great black
mound, formed of immense quantities
of cinders, ashes, and animal and vege-
table refuse, collected from the surrounding parishes. The stench con-
tinually issuing from the enormous
mass of decaying matter was unendur-
able. Fever, and every other disease
were never absent from the crime-
stained locality, which was chiefly in-

habited by starving weavers, thieves,
courtesans, prize-fighters, and dog
stealers.

It was characteristic of the Baroness
that she should have picked out this
Ultima Thule of poverty and degradation for the site of a new and noble
enterprise, which, as in the case of so
many other of her efforts, led directly
to a far reaching and beneficent improvement in the condition of the poor
of London. This spot was chosen for
the erection of four blocks of model
dwellings for the poor, the first buildings of the kind, and those upon which
the Peabody buildings, and many other
model lodging-houses, were afterward
designed. The reeking mass of refuse
was speedily removed, and by May,
1862, Columbia Square was in exist-
ence, affording accommodation for
two hundred families, or about a thousand persons. Each house contains
forty-five complete tenements, generally consisting of two, and sometimes

of three rooms, one of which is provided with a good kitchen range. Re-
membering the habits of the class
from which the tenants would be
drawn, special attention was paid to
secure abundant light and ventilation.
Excellent drainage, lavatories, and
baths, gave advantages to the inhabitants not at that time enjoyed by persons in much more favored circumstances, and at the top of each building was fitted an excellent laundry.
A reading room and library of five
hundred standard volumes were also
provided.

It is rarely indeed that a pioneer
effort anticipates to such a remarkable
extent its own future development.
These buildings, however, were so far
in advance of the standard of that day
that even now they are able to bear
comparison with others recently
erected, and designed to meet the requirements of the latest developments
of sanitary science. They were im-

mediately occupied, and have ever
since been eagerly sought after ; among
the tenants, drunkenness and disease
in great measure disappeared, and an
almost Dutch - like cleanliness and
tidiness are everywhere to be observed

VII.

COLUMBIA MARKET.

THE erection of the Columbia Square
model dwellings was soon followed
by a work of much greater importance
Columbia Market was begun in 1864,
the object in view being to secure for
the poor of the district an abundant
supply of cheap and wholesome food.
The consumer, it was hoped, might be
brought into more immediate communication with the producer, and an
open square of the market was designed as a refuge for the costermongers, who, it was announced, were
about to be driven from the streets by
a new police regulation. As the work
progressed many rumors were rife as
to the exact amount of the expenditure
so lavishly being incurred by Miss

Burdett - Coutts, and as it drew nearer
completion the people were astonished
at the beauty and elegance of the pile.
The best description possible will be
that which appeared in the *Times* when
the market was opened, some technical
details only being omitted: " The
gift which is offered to the poorest
part of that poor neighbourhood is
Miss Burdett - Coutts' new market, a
market which has been built by her
during the last four years at a cost
of more than two hundred thousand
pounds, a market the like of which for
lavish decoration and almost extrava-
gant adornment, does not exist in
the world   The Halles of Paris and
the Central Market of Brussels are
as nothing when compared with the
beauty of this almost cathedral
pile.   We say cathedral pile advisedly,
for it was only the other day when a
Right Rev. prelate came to see the
Central Hall, which bears a strong
resemblance to the side aisles of West-

minster Abbey, he said all it wanted
was a pulpit to carry out the notion
that visitors were in the nave of a fine
church. It is really impossible to over-
value the beauty of the whole structure,
or the skill with which a magnificent
series of buildings has been adapted to
the every‑day wants of a market, of
dwelling houses, and cheap lodging
houses. Wherever one turns there is
something to attract the eye and please
the taste. The gates are masterpieces
of scroll wrought‑iron work. The
corridors are roofed with carved groined
arches of polished teak. Every pillar
is of polished granite, and the capital
of every pillar is a little carved chapter
of ornament in itself . . , All, down
even to the smallest details, whether
it is a side gateway or a door to a cel-
lar, are equally elaborate in their way.
Rich carvings in polished granite meet
the eye at every turn, with towers, and
belfries, and pointed arches, carved
deeply with appropriate texts from

8

Scripture.   It is in the Hall, however,
that what may fairly be said to be the
glories of the architecture culminate:
This Hall, like the rest of the buildings,
is in what is called the Second Pointed
Style, that is to say the most beautiful
period of the 14th century.   The cross
pointed roof is a perfect specimen of
careful woodwork, and the clusters of
polished granite columns which support
it are in similar style to the Chapter
House in Salisbury, only twice as lofty;
indeed we believe they are more lofty
even than the central columns of the
Chapter House of Westminster . . .
With its quaint carved gables and gar-
goyles, its rich Gothic lamps, its spires
and pinnacles, its tall pointed windows,
its tower and open belfry, it resembles
such a building as we should expect to
find in Oxford rather than in the
centre of the poorest parts of Bethnal
Green.   From the carved doorway by
which you enter, up to the topmost
finials of the beautiful clock tower, all

is finished with the careful minuteness of a painting, or what is perhaps even higher praise, with the conscientious labour of the Gothic sculptors of old. The Hall, exclusive of its cellars, is only one story high, and it measures a little over 100 feet in length by 50 feet in width and 50 feet high. The space in the centre, affording an area of about 2,600 superficial feet, is unobstructed by fixtures of any kind, as it is intended for the accommodation of small dealers, but in the aisles, immediately behind the pillars, are ranged 24 small shops. A clock tower and belfry rise to the height of 115 feet. The market yard covers about 8,000 superficial feet, and in it carts will unload and most of the wholesale business of the market be carried on, so that the retail traffic, which, from the character of the neighbourhood, is likely to be the most important, will not be interfered with in any way. The buildings on the East and West sides of the quad-

rangle are similar in design, and con-
sist of five rows of shops with a lofty
central archway in the midst. There
is a coffee shop and a tavern, with all
the usual buildings, such as houses for
clerks of the market, watchmen's
houses, etc. The arcades on each side
of the gate house, which faces South,
are closed in by exquisitely designed
wrought iron gates . . . each arcade,
too, being supplied with a granite
washing fountain, the basin of which
is six feet in diameter. The market
buildings have been designed to meet
as far as possible the requirements of
five different classes of occupiers, viz.,
city clerks who will occupy fourteen
residences; first class dealers who will
occupy twelve large shops and residences in the East and West buildings ;
second class dealers who will occupy
twenty-four small shops and offices in
the Market Hall; third class dealers
who will occupy two hundred and seventy-three spaces six feet square

on the ground floor, in the galleries of
the Market Hall, and in the South Arcades; and lastly, fourth class dealers
who will occupy four hundred spaces, six
feet square, in the central quadrangle. "

Such was the building which Miss
Burdett - Coutts raised on the site of
Nova Scotia Gardens. The opening
ceremony was performed amid a great
popular demonstration on Wednesday,
April 28, 1869, and was attended by
H.R.H. the Duchess of Cambridge,
the Duke and Duchess of Teck, the
Archbishop of Canterbury, the Bishop
of London, and the Lord Mayor and
Sheriffs. Several addresses were presented to the Foundress, and among
them one from the workmen employed.
In acknowledging this on Miss Burdett-
Coutts' behalf, the Archbishop said
that though he might be wrong, he
believed it was unusual for London
landlords and tenants to meet in the
same relations as those which characterized the meeting between Miss Bur-

dett-Coutts and her tenants that day
Miss Burdett-Coutts hoped that the
same good feeling would always pre-
vail, and, apart from the beauty of the
market, she rejoiced at the reconstruction of a neighborhood which, from
combined circumstances, had fallen
into dilapidation and squalor.

It would be outside the scope of this
volume to attempt to explain the reason why this market scheme, beneficent in its conception and located in
such a superb building, was not attended with the hoped-for results. To
do so it would be necessary to ex-
amine the state of the food supply
of London, the conditions of the
wholesale and retail methods of distribution, and especially the strength
and extent of what was known as
the "Ring," controlling the former
department of trade. Suffice it to say
—on the subject of one department
only, the fish supply—that with the
seas around the British islands teem-

ing with wholesome food, and with a population of five millions of people eager to obtain such food at reasonable prices, the supply was choked, so to speak, in the narrow neck of a bottle, represented by a single market for all London. The vested interests connected with that market controlled the supply with an iron hand by means of the system of mortgages on the fishermen's boats all round the coast. The "Ring" rose in alarm at what threatened to be a serious invasion of their monopoly, and eventually, in spite of repeated efforts, and after a marked success in supplying the poorer inhabitants of the district, as well as offering new facilities for trade to the retail dealers, the supplies dwindled away and were finally cut off at their source.

It was hardly possible for the Baroness alone and unaided to engage in a great trade, or to undertake the actual business of supplying London with food. She had observed the crying

need for, and had supplied a new
machinery of, distribution. This she
now proceeded to transfer as a free
gift to the Corporation and City of
London, the only condition being that
they should endeavor to promote the
objects for which the market was established. But the vested interests
already alluded to were all-powerful
among its new owners, and no attempt
of any kind was made to utilize the
market. In 1874 the Lord Mayor of
London wrote to the Baroness, report-
ing an opinion of the Common Council,
that though the Corporation had an
unexpired term of two years in which
to test the possibility of making Columbia Market successful, yet it was felt to
be unfair to every interest concerned,
and therefore undesirable, for the Corporation to continue the experiment
without first consulting her ladyship
as to a re-transfer of the market to her.
The Baroness in reply said she understood from the resolution that the Cor-

poration prior to any further dealing
with the market offered to restore it to
her if she desired to resume the possession of it, in the hope that she
might be able to carry out her original
plans. Her best thanks were due to
them for the frankness and courtesy
with which they had treated her in
making this offer Inasmuch as she
still had a great hope that she might
be able to effect her object, she would
follow the example set her by the Corporation, and frankly at once accept
the offer of the Corporation to re-transfer the market to her, in order that
she might make another attempt to
carry out successfully her original intentions The concluding part of this
letter, it is reported, was "received
with much cheering."

An effort was then made to induce
the railway companies, who were greatly hampered by the crowded ap-
proaches to Billingsgate, to make use
of Columbia. Billingsgate had been

built for a waterside market when railway communication did not exist, and
it was hopéd that the position of Columbia would offer great advantages
for the reception of railway-borne fish.
But it is notoriously difficult to change
the course of trade, and at the first
opposition from the existing center the
railway companies abandoned the enterprise. Again in 1884 Mr. Burdett-
Coutts re-opened the building as a fish
market, and maintained it for two
years, during which time a large business was done. In spite of deter-
mined opposition he succeeded in get-
ting an Act of Parliament, enabling
the railways to run into the market;
but by this time the whole question
of market accommodation had been
opened up and the railway companies
were bent on establishing separate de-
pôts of supply on their own property.
Mr. Burdett-Coutts had based his plan
entirely on the co-operation of the
railway companies, and feeling that

the enterprise was too colossal for any private individual to carry out alone, he reluctantly desisted from the attempt.

That this magnificent structure remains at the present moment without its original object having been carried to a material or practical issue, is true. But it has more than once been pointed out in these pages that the greatest effect of the Baroness' work has often been achieved by means of suggestion and example. So unquestionably it has been with Columbia. The building of the market, the efforts made to carry it on, the bitter opposition that it excited in certain quarters, concentrated general attention upon the subject. Public opinion, effectually aroused, demanded new markets and a widening of the channels of distribution. New markets were then established; but, as already pointed out, these, too, fell more or less under the control of vested interests. This, al-

though an improvement, was no solu-
tion of the real difficulty. Finally a
Royal Commission was appointed, and
the evidence laid before it amply
proved the case which the Baroness
had originally set forth, and on behalf
of which she had made such efforts.
Legislation on the subject has not yet
taken definite form, but the recom-
mendations of the Royal Commission
plainly indicate that it will be framed
on lines identical in spirit and purpose
with those which led to the building of
Columbia Market.

VIII.

IRELAND.

L ADY Burdett-Coutts' bounty in
Ireland has extended over so long
a period that it is difficult now to obtain precise information as to the work
of early years. The results attained,
the gradual and apparently spontaneous raising of the standard of life's ideal
among a whole population, are also of
a more intangible character than those
usually pointed at as the sign of successful philanthropy. Throughout her
career, one of her chief aims has
been to remove the able and energetic
from the unfavorable environment in
which they have been placed by ad-
verse circumstances, but, that done, to
leave them to achieve success largely
by their own exertions. In the words

of Mr. Burdett-Coutts, addressed to a
deputation of the Harbor Board of Skibbereen, "her earnest wish has always
been that whatever she did should not
be of a finite but of a reproductive
character, improving the moral as well
as the material condition of those whom
she assisted." And nowhere has this
principle been attended with such
happy results as in the South-West
corner of Ireland.

The sphere of this portion of her
ladyship's operations has been the district from Skibbereen to Crookhaven,
and in the opposite direction from Skibbereen to the furthest of the Islands,
including Sherkin, Hare, Cape Clear,
and the Calves. She had responded
to an appeal from that district even before the famine year, but did not become closely identified with it until
1862. It had enjoyed a fairly prosperous record up to 1848, probably
owing to the fact that the population,
though numerous, did not rely exclu-

sively upon the soil for a means of livelihood. Around them was the harvest of the sea which some of them occasionally gathered with the help of the primitive fishing-craft they then possessed. But the years 1848 and 1849 brought with them untold misery. Nets, gear, and boats, all went in the competition for food. The bread-winners themselves perished, and a correspondent who visited Cape Clear shortly afterwards found that a couple of " hookers," and some rowing boats, were all that remained of what had been a respectable fleet. From that time forward the history of the district was one of chronic want, occasionally deepening into famine.

It was in the year 1862 that the Rev. Father Leader, the Catholic priest in charge of the parish of Rathmore, or Rath (now known as Baltimore, County Cork), addressed an appeal to Miss Burdett-Coutts. A story is told, and is apparently true, that this appeal was

the result of a series of coincidences.
A workman in Paris, after listening to
a sermon in aid of the suffering Irish,
placed in the collection bag a silver
watch and a ring. The articles were
sent to Father Leader, and, in a raffle,
realized fifty pounds. On hearing the
news, Mr. Leonard, who had forwarded
the articles from Paris, made arrangements during the autumn for a greater
" drawing " in Ireland, to which the
Empress of the French contributed
valuable prizes. It was during his presence in Ireland then that Mr. Leonard
one day tossed across the table to
Father Leader a letter addressed to
Miss Burdett-Coutts suggesting that
the priest should sign it. Laughingly
disregarding it at the time, Father
Leader afterwards signed and des-
patched the letter. This story is confirmed by the fact that the body of the
letter received by Miss Burdett-Coutts
is certainly not in the hand-writing of
Father Leader who signed it.

Whatever may have been the circumstances prompting the good priest, his appeal received a generous response. A commissioner, Mr. W. H. Wills, one of Miss Burdett-Coutts' most trusted advisers, a distinguished literary man and the life-long friend of Charles Dickens, was appointed to visit the district. By the 31st of October, 1862, his report was in the hands of Miss Burdett-Coutts. " I have finished my commission," he said, "and have witnessed a degree and amount of misery which I could not have believed compatible with human life."

Mr. Willis passed through the Island of Sherkin, and visited the mainland, but was not able to get to Clear Island without the risk, which it was unadvisable to incur, of being detained there by unfavorable weather for some weeks. The exceptional distress was due to the failure of the harvest, the "fanatical repugnance" of the people to enter the workhouse, and the absence

9

of any system of out-door relief. " The
squalor and destitution I beheld," he
says, " can hardly be exceeded.   Cabins are built of stones without mortar,
covered with rotten thatch, nearly all
without windows, and some with no
chimneys, thick layers of manure inter-
spersed with puddles of fetid water
lie before the doors ; " while within the
better cabins the furniture consisted of
a long wooden box on legs, a chair or
two, and a bank of salted fish under
ragged tarpaulins.   He speaks of the
wan faces and emaciated frames of
children, who had not tasted food during the preceding day.   "A sick tailor
had fasted since the previous morning.
He was in bed ; his wife and four children seated beside the hearth hungrily
waiting while the eldest daughter
ground and cooked a little borrowed
barley at some green flameless furze,
emitting nothing but smoke.   This
group, with a woman whose husband
and four children had nothing what-

ever to eat, and no bed to lie upon but straw, were among the most affecting objects I encountered.

"Except two, all I spoke to were heavily in debt. I wondered who could trust them; but fifty per cent. above the market price is systematically exacted from them. Two or three persons sign a joint 'We O. U.', not only for the price of the meal, but for interest in advance." In conclusion, Mr. Wills added: "A fishery, properly organized, would produce competence."

This valuable and interesting report was submitted by Miss Burdett-Coutts to Sir Robert Peel, who said that its accuracy was confirmed by the Government weekly returns. He promised special attention to the matter, but expressed the opinion that the chronic destitution could only be met by capital, and by new kinds of enterprise changing the cotters into laborers. Sir Robert issued directions to the Poor Law authorities at Skibbereen as to

out-door relief, and suggested to Miss
Burdett-Coutts the establishment on
Clear Island and Sherkin of a little
store for meal and fuel, with a few
blankets for the sick and aged.

In January, 1863, a party of emigrants was sent out from Sherkin to
Canada, at Miss Burdett-Coutts' expense, there being no authority under
which the Guardians could assist such
a scheme by contributions from the
rates.   On the news of their arrival
being received, a second party was
organized and sent out in April, the
distress having then been aggravated by
the decision of the traders to refuse further credit.   The preparations attending the departure of the second party
were placed in the hands of Mr. John
Sapsford, who, among other instructions, was directed by Miss Burdett-
Coutts to "keep strictly to charity.   I
can have nothing to do with local or
denominational questions.   Heal dif-
ferences if possible."

A third party of emigrants followed,
and Sir Henry Becher, the owner of
much of the land in the district,
expressed his readiness to give facilities for deep sea fishing, though he did
not think the people would be able to
work a fishery successfully without the
assistance of English captains, for
whom he was ready to build comfortable cottages. The native population,
he said, were "neither skilful nor
energetic fishermen," and Mr. O'Dono-
van, the chairman of the Bandon and
Skibbereen Railway, also thought, with
many others, "You could not have
sufficient confidence in the people to
let them have large boats for deep-sea
fishing.

By various little expedients Miss
Burdett - Coutts hoped to succeed in
permanently raising the people from
their then state of degradation and
despair. Sir Joseph Hooker, the distinguished botanist at Kew, was
consulted as to the possibility of intro-

ducing into the country other vegetables by which the potato might be
partly replaced. An energetic attempt
was made, under the patronage of the
Queen, to promote the sale in London
of Irish embroidered handkerchiefs.
But the autumn of 1863, with a ruined
potato crop, was followed by a winter
as wretched as any ever known. The
stores suggested by Sir Robert Peel,
therefore, were opened at Sherkin and
at Clear Island, with supplies of corn,
flour, meal, sugar, and tea, to be sold
at such prices as the people could
afford to pay, and with a supply of
blankets which were to be lent or given
to deserving applicants. The promo-
tion of Father Leader at this time
threw the chief responsibility of this
work on the Rev. J. Allen, the Protest-
ant Rector of Creagh.

Considerable difficulty was experienced the following year in inducing
the people to realize that Miss Burdett-
Coutts did not intend opening a gen-

eral store for gratuitous relief, and in making them clearly understand that she required those who could afford it to pay for the goods supplied. She wrote a letter, therefore, to be read to the people, clearly indicating the principles upon which she wished her work in Ireland to be conducted.

"I sincerely hope the efforts made to prevent the demoralizing effects of aid and help, may be secured by avoiding *gratuitous* distribution of food, money or clothes. Sometimes such distribution may be rendered necessary from sickness, abject poverty, or the pressure when the season is severe, and such has been the cause, I presume, of the large amount of gratuitous assistance which seems to have taken place with respect to the stores provided by me in Ireland, which has produced the result that these stores require replenishing without any means towards doing so being provided by the sale of the articles. I shall be happy to come forward again ; but I should wish it understood that I do so on the condition that the attempt should be conscientiously made to make the stores pay, or at least clear the expenses. I should inflict a considerable injury on all classes at Skibbereen and the Islands if I adopted a different course. It is difficult to do everything right at first, and the first thing certainly was to save life, and afford relief.

"I think a further step should now be taken, and it would be well to explain to the people why such gratuitous assistance cannot continue. It would be, in my opinion, quite an insult to the hard - working, willing islanders, to be treated as mendicants, and also it would injure the property and the place. My object is not to make dependents on my bounty, or on that of any one else, but to bring them comforts which can be secured by their own industry hereafter."

Matters proceeded on a somewhat better basis for some time after this, and in the spring, the crops promising well and the demands having greatly fallen off, the stores were closed ; being subsequently re-opened only as an ordinary shop in the charge of an old pensioner.

Sir Robert Peel, after visiting the islands in 1865 established a post and regular communication between Clear Island and the mainland, and provided improved harbor accommodation. Miss Burdett-Coutts introduced a flock of sheep there, and still persisted in her efforts to create a demand for Irish embroidery. She also provided some small sums of money for the purchase of nets and boats, supplied vats and drying sheets, and gave other encouragement to an attempt to establish a trade in cured fish and nets. She provided a cart, for transporting over-land boats that could not beat their way out of the long narrow creeks and indentations characteristic of the coast, and she gave clothing and assistance to the inhabitants of Hare Island when their homes were destroyed by fire.   Model cottages would also have been built there, but for the insuperable difficulties raised, in their ignorance, by the people it was intended to benefit.   Of the suitable sites one was said to be haunted, and another was too close to a "Killeen"—the burial place of children dying unbaptized.   Another was objected to on the ground that it "crossed the ridge," or in other words ran at right angles to the furrows, which was considered "unlucky." Many of these people were afterwards sent to Canada.

Work of this character (though there is no need to recapitulate details) was quietly continued during the following years.   A certain amount of enterprise had been stimulated, and several of the men had borrowed money with which to purchase larger boats. Unfortunately in more than one instance they hopelessly handicapped themselves by borrowing this money from small professional usurers at twenty-five per cent. per annum, though as the same men afterwards discovered they could procure the accommodation from the Bank at six per cent. In these early efforts they also met with exceptional disaster by losing gear, nets, etc., in unusually severe weather. Several such cases coming under the notice of the Baroness she felt justified in granting aid either in relieving them from part of their incumbrances, or in supplying new gear. Much distress was also caused in 1879 by the extraordinary outbreak at Cape Clear of German measles, to which adults were especially subject, and from which they suffered severely. A priest in charge wrote, "The disease was introduced from Skull (where it wore a very favourable aspect) by a woman of the Island. Her husband, her brother, and

her sister, and about seventeen from
that particular townland, were attacked,
and *without exception died*. Since then
about thirty-five others are struggling
with the disease. The bread winners
have been destroyed—in one family
five places made vacant. This scourge
has made many a house where peace
and comfort reigned but a short time
ago, desolate and wretched to-day."

The Baroness remitted a considerable sum to her agent on the spot, and
suggested an appeal to the general
public. Sisters of charity went to
nurse the sick, and a temporary hospital was provided by the Board of
Trade.

Her Ladyship was also a subscriber
to, and a supporter of, the fund started
in 1881 for the relief of Irish ladies in
distress through non-payment to them
of the rent of their small properties,
or of annuities or mortgage-interest.
Among this class distress was very

severe, and not the less real because it was endured in silence. It was found that a considerable number of such persons, having previously lived in comfort, were reduced by the default of their debtors to want even the means of subsistence.

This section of the Baroness' Irish work may be well closed by the record of a munificent offer, made to the Government in 1880, suggested to her Ladyship by Mr. Burdett-Coutts (then Mr. W. Ashmead-Bartlett) who made a tour of the counties of Sligo, Mayo, and Roscommon, and prepared a careful report on the condition of the peo-- ple who were suffering severely owing to the failure of the potato crop. The tremendous rainfalls saturating the boglands had also made the peat useless, and deprived the people of their ordinary fuel. Matters were further aggravated by the falling off of emigration, and by the large number of men, usually required for harvest oper-

ations in England, who were left unemployed owing to the bad season.
Immediate temporary relief was distributed, and, as a measure of permanent improvement, it was proposed, first
to supply new and better seed for some
forty thousand acres; and secondly, to
devise a means of freeing, at any rate,
some of the people, all heavily in debt,
from the whole, or part, of their incumbrances.

The scheme was laid before the
Right Honorable W. H. Smith (then
First Lord of the Admiralty), by the
Baroness, and is more fully explained
by the following letter written by him
to her on February 8, 1880.

" I have been entirely occupied since
I saw you this afternoon with the consideration of your most munificent
proposal.

"Its magnitude and goodness deprived me of the power at the time of
expressing my sense of the pity and
charity which prompted it.

" But I do not feel at liberty to mention it to my colleagues until I have first of all stated to you what I understand it to be:— viz., a gift of a sum not to exceed two hundred and fifty thousand pounds to be applied, in the first instance, to the purchase of seed for destitute tenantry in the distressed districts in Ireland, and repayment being obtained after the harvest, to be then applied in relieving these poor people from the debts by which they are oppressed. I have told you that the Government is engaged in devising a scheme by which the seed shall be lent to the people, and there may be great difficulty in carrying out any plan for the redemption of usurious debts, or preventing them from being incurred again.

" But the sum and the idea are so vast that I should wish to know if I am right before I open my lips.

"Meanwhile I shall see the officers of the Irish Government who will be

in London in the morning to assist in
working out our scheme, which I
sketched out to you, and I shall also
see Mr. Bartlett if he calls upon me.

"If you tell me I have rightly inter-
preted your intentions I will mention
them to my colleagues."

In reply to this letter the Baroness
wrote:—

" My proposal was to advance such
a sum as would secure (humanly speaking) the present and future harvests in
Ireland, upon some plan of repayment,
and with assistance for its distribution
which I thought Government might
secure to me.

"After the harvest question, the most
vital question seemed to me the debts
of the people, and I proposed to relieve
these, if practicable. I don't know I
should be justified in undertaking to
spend the whole of the money advanced for seed when repaid; for circumstances may change, and in any
case some permanent scheme would

have to be devised to prevent, or at
least hinder, the recurrence of this
fatal habit. The sum required for seed
I understood would probably be, but
not exceed, two hundred and fifty
thousand pounds."

Reference has already been made to
the condition of the fishing population,
and to the efforts made by individual
members, to avail themselves of the
wealth which nature had placed at
their disposal around the coast, and
though these efforts were in more than
one instance unwisely directed, there
can be nothing but praise for the spirit
of enterprise by which they were
prompted.

The story of the fishery industry in
Ireland, especially since the date of the
great famine, is a story of neglected
resources. The coast teems with fish,
and yet till recently little was con-
sumed, and none exported. Of the
dried fish bought in Ireland, ten thou-

sand tons a year were imported, much
of which had been caught off the Irish
coasts, and a considerable amount of
which had actually been cured in Ireland itself by Scotch people. Tens of
thousands of fishermen from Great
Britain, France, Norway, and Holland,
made a prosperous living from the Irish
fisheries, while Ireland, with a population of five millions, and a coast line of
two thousand miles, has only twenty
thousand men engaged in the business.
Finally, although there was an enormous demand, both by natives and
foreign visitors for nets, lines, sails, and
shipwrights' work, the coast populations were, and are still, completely
ignorant of the ordinary maritime
trades; the demand for such articles
on the South and South-West coasts of
Ireland having been met from the Isle
of Man and from Scotland.

Galway Bay has been swarming with
herrings for weeks at a time, and a
fortune might have been made by any

who, with boats and gear, were able to
follow the fish out to sea. But there
were no such suitable boats, and with
tons of fish in their own waters the
people of the western towns were eating their potatoes with herrings salted
in Scotland. When in Dungarvan Bay
large quantities of pilchards were
thrown overboard, the Fishery Inspector could only report that " the want
of demand for this fish in a fresh state
renders the fishermen *desirous not to capture*," though pilchards are in great demand in Italy, and are a regular source
of wealth to the Cornishmen. Every
year the people saw their own means of
subsistence carried off before their faces,
while they perforce remained helpless.

The cause lay partly in the want of
general training and of habits of sus-
tained effort, but chiefly in want of
capital. Boats were wanted; big boats of
thirty or forty tons, costing from three
hundred to six hundred pounds each.

It was in these circumstances that

the Baroness intervened, and began in
1879, by assisting men, able to find
some small part of the purchase money,
in buying such boats. Afterwards her
ladyship's agent was instructed to suggest the formation of small companies
among the men, each of whom would
have a share in a boat ; half the purchase money being advanced by the
Baroness while the builders allowed the
men time for payment of the balance.
This tentative effort was attended with
results so encouraging that in 1880 a
sum of ten thousand pounds was placed,
by the Baroness and Mr. Burdett-Coutts
jointly, at the disposal of the Parish
Priest, the Rev. Father C. Davis, who
was assisted by Mr. Sapsford, as a fund
from which similar loans might be made
to men of good character. No security
was required and no interest, all that was
demanded being an installment of ten
per cent. per annum in repayment of the
advance, the amount returned being
available again for the same good work.

It is most gratifying to learn that
the greater part of the money was
faithfully repaid, and as a measure of
the success of the experiment it may be
mentioned that in Baltimore, five years
afterwards, the fishing plant was valued
at fifty thousand pounds. The honor of
the people was felt by themselves to be
staked on the punctual observance of
their engagements, and this feeling was
carefully fostered by Father Davis,
to whose great energy, prudence, and
sound sense, the success of the work
is in a very large measure due. He
knew his people, their virtues and their
failings. In his early letters he says:
"I fully concur in your observations
on the improvidence of the people; no
honest impartial Irishman can deny it.
But it was hard for them within a
short time to become thrifty, and self-
reliant; they must actually be educated into it, especially the secluded
Islanders." Again, he mentions that
they had no example before them of

successful enterprise, and thought it
sufficient to eke out a miserable exis-
tence as their fathers did before them.
"All this I hope will soon pass away; it
shall be my constant endeavor to teach
them to rely upon their own industry
and perseverance." And his word
was faithfully kept. The people were
successfully placed in an improved
position, and escaped the pauperization
which so often attends such efforts.
There was but one attempt made under
the vigilant rule of such a steward to
evade payment of installments. On
hearing of this the strong minded
priest wrote: "I was beside myself
with indignation. On Sunday next, in
the presence of the entire Island, after
divine service, your letter to me will be
publicly read, as well as X----'s to the
Baroness. The stamp of lasting repro-
bation will thus be placed upon him,
and I hope the effect it will have, will
be to make a better and wiser man of
him." The next Sunday an address

in condemnation of the defaulter's
action was signed by the congregation
and forwarded to the Baroness, the of-
fender stepping forward and asking
pardon of his assembled neighbors.
That installment, and all succeeding
ones were promptly paid.

The industry grew apace. Baltimore
became a formidable rival to Kinsale,
the payments for mackerel there to
natives and strangers sometimes reach-·
ing the high figure of ten thousand
pounds in a single week. Its harbor,
formerly deserted, was soon frequented
by four hundred boats. Beside material
prosperity such as that, there was no
room for political agitation by which
the district has ever since remained unaffected.

The Baroness first visited the neighborhood for which she had done so
much in the year 1884, accompanied
by Mr. Burdett-Coutts. She was
known there, years before she had any

legal right to the title, as "*Lady*
Coutts,*"* and occasionally as "Your
Lordship, Lady Coutts," but by the
date of her visit she was generally alluded to as "the Queen of Baltimore."
Certainly it was a royal welcome that
the people gave to their generous bene-
factress, and it need hardly be said
that what she saw there, and the welcome accorded to her, were most gratifying to her. The Baroness recognized around her the proofs of much
good already accomplished, and the
rich promise of greater good yet to result from past effort. The following
extract from a conversation her ladyship had with a newspaper correspondent will no doubt be read with interest as showing her impressions of
the condition of a neighboring part
of Ireland—a condition from which,
at that time, Baltimore had begun to
emerge:

"There is everywhere," she said "to
the most cursory observer, an inde-

scribable lassitude which appears to
hang over all—children, peat, crops,
goats, men and women, animate and in-
animate nature. The country seems
to be perishing from itself, and stands
sorely in need of means of locomotion
and intercourse. The man who lives by
himself, for himself, with no ties outside
himself, on his plot of ground, even
when surrounded by animal comforts,
lacks that motive power for improvement which is created on the one hand
by competition and comparison, and
on the other by community of interest.
He can but hug his eccentricities
with a depressing certainty that his
children—the only things, possibly, he
unselfishly loves—have no other prospect before them."

It was soon after this visit that an
effort was made to render permanent
the work so successfully begun, and to
provide means by which its benefits
would be almost automatically repro-
duced on other parts of the coast. A

scheme for the establishment of a
Fishery Training School for boys, first
suggested by Sir John Letaigne in
1871, was discussed and adopted.
The Baroness contributed material financial assistance, and was an indefati-
gable advocate of the institution in
official and other quarters. The subscription lists were rapidly filled.
Among others the Grand Jury of the
County of Cork subscribed one thous-
and pounds, the Duke of Norfolk sent
a cheque for five hundred pounds ; a
legacy of five hundred pounds was bequeathed, and the Government also
made a grant of five thousand five hundred pounds. By the year 1887 the Baltimore Industrial Fishery School was
erected, and ready to receive its pupils.

The objects of the promoters were
to receive boys from every part of
Ireland, and give them the best instruction possible in every subject connected with the fisherman's craft. In
the School they would learn the theory

of navigation, and on the Atlantic itself would learn to manage the well-found boats belonging to the institution. They would be taught the arts of sail-making, net and rope making, carpentering, coopering, and boat building, and also the important art of curing the fish when caught. These objects are now being satisfactorily pursued. From this School many of the boys, it is hoped, will return to their homes and replace with the new and better methods they have been taught, the primitive fishing of their neighbors. As a proof of its probable influence it may be mentioned that the opening ceremony was attended by a clergyman from Clogerhead, near Drogheda, who went with the express object of acquiring information likely to be of benefit to the fishermen of that district.

The School building, designed to accommodate four hundred boys, is a plain, stone structure, with a simple frontage of concrete, standing on some

rising ground at the back of the village
of Baltimore and overlooking the sea.

The opening ceremony was performed by the Baroness Burdett-Coutts
on the 16th of August, 1887. Her
ladyship who, accompanied by Mr.
Burdett-Coutts and a party of friends,
arrived on board the yacht Pandora,
generously placed at her disposal by
the Right Hon. W. H. Smith, was
again received with enthusiasm. All
down the coast from Queenstown to
Baltimore, flags and strips of colored
cloth, and even tattered handkerchiefs,
fluttered from every house and cottage ;
the people gathered in crowds on every
headland. As the vessel glided at night
into the still lake-like harbor a hundred small fires twinkling far and near
on the wild hill sides, signaled a welcome that was repeated in the booming
of a salute from the shore. On the mor-
row, the village being gorgeous with a
display of bunting, the formality of
opening the Schools was performed.

Numerous addresses were at the same
time presented to her ladyship by various public bodies. In the course of
her remarks, looking back on the past
—"a past which has so many sorrow-
ful pictures,"—and then turning to the
future, the Baroness declared she saw
much reason for hopefulness. "It was
grateful and pleasant," she said, "to
look back to the good that had been
done ; but they had from that day to
look forward to the time when there
ought to be there a lucrative and profitable employment, which, though
humble, would carry wealth to many
poor doors." Such was her hope in
connection with that institution. Her
ladyship concluded by saying:—"I now
declare that this School for all the purposes for which it is intended—and
God grant that they may be fulfilled—
is open."

It only remains to add that to-day
(1893) the school is rapidly justifying
the hopes formed for it at that time.

IX.

IN TIME OF WAR.

THE unfortunate victims of war, combatants and non-combatants, have alike shared the sympathy and generosity of the Baroness. To the Crimea she sent patent drying sheds in which the men exposed to the weather that first dreadful winter might dry their soddened clothes after their spell of duty. She was actively interested in the welfare of our soldiers in Zululand in 1879; and she founded and conducted the Turkish Compassionate Fund by which thousands of lives were saved during the last Russo-Turkish war. At the time of the Soudan expedition the Baroness provided house accommodation for the wives and families of the Cold-

stream Guards when the men were
sent abroad.

The Stafford House South African
Aid Committee was formed in June,
1879, with the object of supplementing
the work of the Government medical
establishments in South Africa, by affording aid to our sick and wounded
soldiers engaged in the war against the
Zulus. A Ladies' Committee was
formed, presided over by the Baroness
Burdett-Coutts, which carefully selected and sent out seven trained
nurses. A great and useful work was
done between June, 1879, and March,
1880, not confined to our own soldiers
but also extended, as mercy demanded,
to the wounded enemy, nearly fifty-five
thousand patients being treated at a
total expenditure of under seven thousand pounds.

The Turkish Compassionate Fund, to
which reference has been made, was a
much greater undertaking. In the story
of the Russo-Turkish war of 1877 the

public is well acquainted with the
charges of cruelty brought against the
Turkish irregular troops engaged in
quelling the rising in Bulgaria. There
was less heard, and there is less remembered, of the suffering endured by
the Turkish populations fleeing before
the approach of the Russians. This
flight of the people was not due to
panic, or to sentimental feelings, which
would probably have had little effect in
inducing them to abandon their homes
and property in a winter when the cold
was so intense (as Mr. Dillon reported
from Rustchuck), that during the night
the wolves ventured up to the house
doors and carried away the watch dogs.
But the people had learned too well by
cruel experience the awful fate—a fate
in which death was the least thing to
be dreaded—awaiting them at the
hands of their Christian neighbors, too
often with the connivance of the Russian troops. It was on behalf of these
people that the Baroness issued her

eloquent appeal in the *Daily Telegraph*, the result of which was the formation of the Turkish Compassionate Fund.

On a theme so revolting, even if space permitted, one is loath to make any detailed reference to the nature of the sufferings of the Turkish population; but one extract from a letter of a British officer may be allowed to describe what may be safely termed the minor cruelties. "I myself have seen and questioned scores of poor women and children who have, though grievously wounded and diabolically outraged, been so far fortunate as to preserve their lives, and they all concur in the statement that vast numbers of their people have been massacred. I spoke yesterday at Rasgrad to an old woman seventy years of age, who had fourteen lance wounds, and had seen her two daughters cruelly outraged and murdered before her eyes. I could multiply instances of Cossack cruelty *ad infinitum*, children who can hardly

II

walk, hacked and prodded with lance
and sabre, and a hundred other iniqui-
ties; but enough has already been said,
and proved, to show how the Christian-
izing Russian legions do their work,
and more than enough to arouse the
generous heart of England to help
these poor destitute creatures before the
cruel Bulgarian winter comes to ex-
pose them to suffering and privations,
which must end in such a hecatomb as
modern Europe has not seen."

As a matter of fact, by the middle
of August, four months after the dec-
laration of war by Russia, the refugees
in the villages of the Danube numbered twenty-nine thousand six hundred and eighty-eight families, and it
was on behalf of these unfortunate victims of the war — non-combatants—
that the Baroness wrote to the editor of
the *Daily Telegraph* the following letter :

"Sir : The accompanying telegram*

* The following is the telegram referred to :
"This war is carried on in a most barbarous way.

was sent in reply to one I forwarded
on Friday to Constantinople for information. The main point to which I
am anxious to direct attention is the
new and good opportunity for the distribution of any funds, which may be
sent direct to the Relief Committee at
Constantinople. His Excellency, our
Minister there, gives his name, a substantial guarantee not only for the

---

Very many fugitives, chiefly Turkish women and
children, who have lost everything in the world and
are starving, and many of whom are provided for
at Adrianople, Varna, and elsewhere. Those in
Constantinople humanely taken care of by the Sultan and principal Turkish families. Committee for
relief of fugitives has been formed at Adrianople,
of which Consul Blunt, the British Vice-Consul,
and other trustworthy people are members, and to
which Mr. Layard gives his name. Money will
be most thankfully received and can be remitted
to Mr. Layard, or Vice-Consul Blunt. The Consul at Varna would also no doubt distribute any
sums. The matter is very urgent, especially at
Adrianople. The description received of the sufferings of these poor creatures is heart-rending.
Amongst them are some Bulgarians and Jews.
Could not the Jewish community do something for
the latter ?"

wise action of the committee organized
by our Consul, Mr. Blunt, and others
of influence, but also for the urgent
need of fresh funds. There are several agencies through which relief to
victims may also be sent, Lady Strang-
ford's Hospital and the Stafford House
Committee, but over and above these
a Compassionate Fund for Turkish
women and children should be, perhaps, now organized. The Society of
Friends having an admirable machinery at command, could act with any
or all of these. The Red Cross and
Crescent Committees might possibly
unite in common action for the suc-
cor of the innocent defenseless sufferers into whose wounds Christendom,
if it is to merit its name, is bound to
pour its oil and its balm. But the call
for help is urgent, and committee
meetings and arrangements in this
country could not meet it so promptly
as would generous relief forwarded at
once to Consul Blunt, or His Excel-

lency Mr. Layard. The latter is the
course I have myself adopted, and
when your vast public reads these few
lines, I trust much bodily or mental
anguish will begin to be soothed
through that real Christianity which is
still, in God's providence, the appointed
means by which hunger and thirst are
assuaged, sickness alleviated, and consolation given. It is unnecessary to
enter more fully into the wants and
sufferings of these cruelly treated Moslems — the daily journals all repeat
them too faithfully — but I would add
a few words to the many who at this
season seek relaxation, health or recreation for themselves and their families,
either by the seaside, on the moors, at
foreign baths, or elsewhere. At all
and each of these resorts whatever can
soften illness or enhance the enjoy-
ments of health will be found. At
this, the beautiful and abundant harvest season, there seems to arise within
us an instinct like that which guides

the swallows to rejoice in the golden
summer, and here, in our own dear
land, we have been in different ways
endeavoring to provide for old and
young, sickly and poor, as well as
rich and strong, some sources of sum-
mer-tide pleasure. It is the season of
God's gifts and goodness to all men,
and it would almost seem as if
the heart of man gladdened in the
smile of heaven as the corn and grain,
hops and the vines, ripen into perfec-
tion for his use. Troubles, sickness,
and sorrow, are cheered by the balmy
influence of air and sunshine, but while
nature tells us to 'rest and be glad,'
I would pray one and all to bear in
mind, either in their travel or their re-
pose, the unhappy sufferers in a far-
away country, of another creed, whose
life is ebbing fast away, uncheered,
desolate, abandoned. We cannot, perhaps, staunch their life blood. We
can wash our own hands, though, free
of its stain by binding up their wounds—

if not by our money, by our sympathy. If silver and gold there is none, we have prayers still, and He to Whom all flesh comes, hears the cry of the poor for His creatures suffering from the sword, as He also accepts the gift of the rich."

This letter touched a chord of national feeling, and, backed up by the powerful advocacy of the *Daily Telegraph* met with an immediate and generous response. The Turkish Compassionate Fund was formed. The Baroness headed the list with one thousand pounds, and in a few days over thirty thousand pounds was received in large and small sums. The rich contributed nobly; columns of the newspapers were required day by day to record the innumerable contributions of the middle class, and all over the country collections were made by those employed in workshops and offices. A large box containing a considerable sum in farthings was mysteriously left with

Messrs. Coutts & Co., the Bankers to the Fund, and a huge store was required in which to warehouse the enormous quantities of clothing, food, and comforts, sent by tradesmen and manufacturers for the refugees.

Mr. Burdett-Coutts (then Mr. Ashmead-Bartlett) appointed Special Commissioner of the Fund, sailed for Constantinople in the yacht "Constance," which was crammed to the decks with stores of medicine, food, and clothing, and proceeded to take charge of operations.

By October bales of clothing were received in Schumla, where the distress was then most severe, and were distributed by Captain Synge. A very large amount of relief was also afforded at Varna, Prevady, Yeni Bazar, and Rasgrad, where many of the people were suffering from small-pox, typhoid, and typhus fever, medical aid being provided and soup kitchens established. As the Russian armies advanced fur-

ther southward the Turkish population sought refuge in Sofia, Phillipop-
olis, and Tatar Bazardjik. At all these
places relief committees were formed
by agents of the Fund, among whom
was Colonel (now Sir Francis) de
Winton, who, in his report on the condition of affairs south of the Balkans
in November, gives the number of
refugees as seventy-three thousand.

The whole of these people, driven
again from the towns just mentioned,
then converged upon Adrianople. Mr.
Burdett-Coutts writing from Tatar
Bazardjik in January, 1878, describes
the scene witnessed there of over two
thousand persons leaving daily in that
terrible cold, traveling in uncovered railway wagons. "Already waiting in vast
crowds at the railway station they are
frozen white, black, and blue. They are
then put into wagons where they wait
in the open air for two or three hours,
and then they are started on their cruel
journey to God knows what suffering."

He suggested the establishment of a
soup kitchen at Adrianople railway
station for feeding the people on
arrival; but before he could reach that
place the Russians had made a sudden
movement upon it by which he was cut
off from headquarters, and was forced
to cross the Rhodope Balkans to the
coast in order to get back to Constantinople, where he organized an immense
system of relief for the new population
of famishing refugees who had entered
the city.

The depôt at Adrianople had been
well set in working order, and as the
crowds poured into the town they were
dealt with as effectively as the circumstances permitted. They then passed
on to Constantinople, the roads to the
capital being crowded with a half-clad,
starving mass, struggling through the
mire with some poor remains of their
portable property. The journey by
rail was even worse, though as the
trains left Adrianople numbers clung to

the outside and framework of the carriages, and many attempted to ride on
the buffers. Women rode on the
roofs of the carriages, till, numbed
with cold, they rolled off in the night
never to be heard of again. Fifteen
were found dead in the trucks in one
morning. Some went mad. Women
were confined, and mothers, as they
crossed the bridge, threw their children
into the river Maritza, preferring to
end their sufferings at once rather than
prolong the cruel horror of that
dreadful journey.

On arrival at Constantinople, they
were received in a refuge, fed and then
distributed in various directions, leaving the place free for the next batch.
The Sultan threw open one of his palaces for the reception of some of these
unfortunates; the wealthy Turkish families also provided for others, and
thousands found shelter in the Mosques.
The work of the Compassionate Fund
in Constantinople in February, 1878,

by which time the Russians were at
the gates, included feeding, housing
and partly clothing three thousand
people; treating four hundred patients
in four hospitals — one of them for
small-pox—giving soup to two thousand and bread to numbers at one time
reaching over twenty thousand daily,
in addition to other and smaller sys-
tems of relief.

The total cost of the operation of
the fund was forty-three thousand
pounds. A small amount was devoted
to an effort to re-settle the people in
their old homes, towards which the Baroness contributed a further sum of one
thousand pounds, but the greatest difficulty was experienced in the work,
and many of the unfortunate Moslems,
claiming their own, were driven out *vi
et armis* by Bulgarians who had seized
their property.

A small balance remaining in hand
at the conclusion of the mission was
devoted to the development of a school

for native embroidery, in which the
women were found to be most skillful.
This school is still most successfully
conducted by its foundress, Mrs. Han-
son, among those so employed being
some who, before the war, held high
social positions.

In recognition of her humane efforts
on behalf of his unfortunate people the
Sultan sent to the Baroness the First
Class and Star of the Order of the
Medjidiyeh, a decoration conferred on
no other woman except Her Majesty
the Queen, and this was followed by
the Grand Cross and Cordon of the
newly established Order of Mercy (the
Shafakat). His Majesty's message,
conveyed through the Foreign Minister to Musurus Pasha, the Turkish
Ambassador in England, was as follows : —

"Our August Master has been much
touched by the kindness and generosity displayed by the Baroness Burdett-
Coutts towards the innocent victims of

the Russian atrocities, and directs you to express his most sincere thanks, not only to that noble lady, but to the other members of the committee instituted through her initiative. The unfortunate refugees themselves will for ever preserve with profound gratitude the memory of these acts of benevolence." The Sultan had already conferred on Mr. Burdett - Coutts the Collar and Star of the Medjidiyeh.

STRAY LEAVES.   175

X.

STRAY LEAVES.

THE foregoing pages have treated
various large and important enterprises of specific kinds with which the
Baroness has been connected, the investigation of which for the purposes
of this volume has offered no special
difficulty. But how is it possible to
trace the innumerable minor channels
along which, for over half a century,
the Baroness has directed her public
and private benevolence? And even
were these traced the sum of the indirect and more remote consequences,
which necessarily remain unknown,
must vastly outweigh the direct and
immediate results which only are
noted. A man some years ago saved
the lives of several children at a fire

in London. It afterwards transpired,
that years before, this man had himself been found, an outcast, by one of
the Baroness' agencies, and by it enabled to lift himself out of his wretched
surroundings. This case, only one of
many, stands as a type. In speaking
here of the work of the Baroness' life
we speak not of work accomplished,
but of an initial power set in operation
by her, the final results of which this
generation has not seen, and will not
see.

One of her earliest efforts was the
establishment of a home for women at
Shepherd's Bush. In this, Charles
Dickens spared neither time nor
trouble. He superintended the purchase of land and buildings, the repairs
and furnishing. He drew up rules,
framed in a broad and truly charitable
spirit, and with a view of making as
easy as might be the new path which
the inmates would strive to follow.

He visited the prisons, and with the help of Governors and Magistrates selected the most hopeful cases. To these he sent an anonymous invitation to start a new life in a home where there would be no harsh or arbitrary rules, no distinctive dress, and no reference to the past. This invitation, which best explains the aim of the institution, is addressed "to a woman," to one who has lived miserably with no prospect before her but sorrow, nothing behind her but "a wasted youth;" and it continues:

" You are such a person, or this letter would not be put into your hands. If you have ever wished (I know you must have done so sometimes) for a chance of rising out of your sad life, and having friends, a quiet home, means of being useful to yourself and others, peace of mind, self respect, everything you have lost, pray read it attentively, and reflect upon it afterwards. I am going to offer you, not the chance but the certainty of all these blessings, if you will exert yourself to deserve them. And do not think that I write to you as if I felt myself very much above you, or wished to hurt your feelings by reminding you of the situation in which you are placed. God forbid! I mean nothing but kindness to you, and I write as if you were my sister.

*   *   *   *

"There is a lady in this town who, from the windows of her house, has seen such as you going past at night, and has felt her heart bleed at the sight. She is what is called a great lady; but she has looked after you with compassion as being of her own sex and nature, and the thought of such fallen women has troubled her. She has resolved to open, at her own expense, a place of refuge very near London for a small number of women, who without such help are lost for ever, and to make it a *home* for them. In this

Home they will be taught all household
work that would be useful to them in a
home of their own, and enable them to
make it comfortable and happy. In
this Home, which stands in a pleasant
country lane, and where each may
have her little flower garden, if she
pleases, they will be treated with the
greatest kindness; will lead an active,
cheerful, healthy life; will learn many
things it is good to know, and, being
entirely removed from all who have any
knowledge of their past career, will begin life afresh, and be able to win a
good name and character. And because it is not the lady's wish that
these young women should be shut out
from the world after they have repented
and have learned how to do their duty
there, and because it *is* her wish and
object that they may be restored to
society, they will be supplied with
every means, when some time shall
have elapsed, and their conduct shall
have fully proved their earnestness

and reformation, to go abroad, where
in a distant country, they may become
the faithful wives of honest men, and
live and die in peace."

This was the work at Urania College,
Shepherd's Bush, and though it was afterwards found advisable to seek as inmates those who had taken only the first
steps in vice, instead of those long
numbered in the ranks of crime, yet
the work had a great and a long success.   By twos and threes, after proba-
tion, the girls were emigrated under
careful supervision, and began the life
which, in many cases, had been
rendered impossible for them by the
force of surrounding circumstances.
For, says Dickens in one of his letters,
"It is dreadful to think how some of
these doomed women have no chance
or choice.   It is impossible to disguise
from oneself the horrible truth that it
would have been a social marvel and
miracle if some of them had been anything else than what they are."

In emigration the Baroness saw at a very early date the best opportunity of effecting permanent improvement in the individual, and in the over-crowded locality from which he was taken. In 1863 she defrayed the expenses of a party of emigrants, over one hundred in number, to Halifax, N. S., writing them, on the eve of their departure, a long letter full of sound advice and excellent suggestions. Among these people were elderly men and women, and children in arms. Many of the younger men had been selected from the St. Giles' Refuge, and several families were taken from the neighborhood of Brown's Lane, East London. Three separate parties were sent out from Ireland under circumstances which have already been mentioned. In 1869 some twelve hundred weavers were sent to Australia from Girvan, Ayrshire, by means of a large loan from Miss Burdett-Coutts, and this is the only unsatisfactory case with which

she was ever connected. The people,
it has been ascertained, not only prospered, but prospered so well that they
sent to their friends at home the means
of joining them. But the loan was not
repaid ; in fact was never afterward
referred to.

The latest effort in this direction
with which the Baroness has been connected, has been an attempt at colonization made by a small private body,
"The London Colonization Aid Society," with a view of proving that
advances made for the purpose of
placing labor on the untilled soil of
Canada, and of assisting it during the
earlier stages of cultivation, may be
considered a profitable investment.
Advances of one hundred pounds have
been made to each family, all these
being purposely selected from East
London; for, though these people,
knowing nothing of agriculture, were
probably the least fit subjects for such
an experiment, they were chosen for

the purpose in order to ascertain the possibilities of success under the most disadvantageous circumstances. A very satisfactory proportion have been successful as agriculturists, others have done well in the towns in trades, and, as anticipated, there have been a few failures. The possibility of the enterprise being successfully conducted, and even conducted on a very large scale under a more strict management, may be considered proved.

Every measure for ensuring to the poor, especially in towns, an abundant supply of cheap food of good quality, has been advocated by the Baroness. It was to further this end that the great market, already described, was built by her in East London. In raising her protest against the conditions of the over-sea live cattle trade, the Baroness also felt that—to use her own words—"the mental and bodily sufferings" of the animals before

slaughter must injuriously affect the
quality of the meat. With a similar
feeling, at the time of the cattle
plague, particularly in 1865, she called
upon the Government to take special
measures to protect the food supply of
the poor; and on every opportunity
she has pointed to the importance of
sound instruction for girls in the art of
cookery. In Westminster, as this volume is being written, an instructor
from the Military School of Cookery
at Aldershot is, at the request of the
Baroness, delivering a course of excellent lectures on the preparation of
nourishing and extraordinarily cheap
meals for the people.

Good food, well cooked, good housing, such as has been provided by her
at Columbia, and then a plentiful supply of pure air,—these the Baroness
would have enjoyed by every inhabi-
tant of our great cities; for they are,
except possibly the last, within the
reach of all. The preservation of

commons, the provision of open spaces
and parks, and, in the more densely
crowded districts, of old churchyards
laid out as gardens, has always had
her support. She very materially assisted in the preservation of the fields
and woodlands adjoining Hampstead
Heath, which now afford to Londoners
a recreation ground of about five hundred acres. This spot, standing higher
than any other environ, and with singu-
lar rural charms, is the pleasure ground
of "poorer London," while the air that
enters the great city from this direction passes over a fresh green upland,
pure and free from the contamination
that it would have carried had this
expanse not been saved from the
builder.

To Hospitals, Orphanages, and Asy-
lums of every kind the Baroness has
been a generous subscriber. To Church
restorations she has often made liberal
donations. To the church at Borough-

bridge, the constituency for which her father, Sir Francis Burdett, was first returned to Parliament, she presented a peal of bells, and she has given separate bells to several other parishes. She has set up large and beautiful fountains and drinking troughs in various parts of the country—in Victoria Park, Columbia Market, and the Zoölogical Gardens in London; in Ancoats, Manchester; and in Edinburgh. She gave two lifeboats to the English Society, and placed a third at St. Malo on the French Coast, that being but one instance of her charitable interest in other lands. She distributed several thousand copies of a French Edition of the "British Workman" under the title of "L'Ouvrier Français," upon which the representatives of the Society of Friends then in France reported that "if that publication could be furnished throughout France regularly, it would be a real boon to the country." In America itself, a contribution from the

Baroness, in aid of the sufferers by the Charleston disaster, was received by cable during the morning on which the catastrophe was reported.

The Baroness has been an intimate friend of Rajah Sir James Brooke, the modern Raleigh, of Dr. Livingstone, Dr. Moffat, General Gordon, and Mr. H. M. Stanley, and was in some measure able to advance their work, which she always followed with the closest attention. In the first of these cases the romantic episode recalls the earliest tales of history. A private English gentleman became a king, and established a dynasty; but the Kingdom of Borneo would never have passed into his hands without the generous aid of the Baroness.

In these, and in many other historic enterprises, she has played a deeply interesting part. After the murder of Bishop Hannington, it will be remembered that his diary found its way to the coast, and was brought to England. Few who were present will forget the touching scene when, at a great meeting in Westminster, the little book worn and stained, and wrapped in brown paper, was placed in her hands, as the most fitting to receive it first in England.

General Gordon, who maintained an almost impenetrable social isolation, valued her friendship, and barely an hour before leaving England for the last time went to see her. Expressing a desire to receive some little memento from her hands, she gave him a letter case which always lay on her table, and it is known that he always carried this about him to the last. Later, when General Gordon was shut up in Khartoum and no effort was made to rescue him, she joined with a few other private friends in engaging an English merchant, resident in Morocco, to undertake the perilous enterprise of finding his way into Khartoum, in disguise, with a packet of letters and English newspapers, which were the last words Gordon ever had from England, and which told him how deeply the national heart was stirred on his behalf.

In this connection it is convenient to refer to one aspect of the Baroness' life which can only be briefly touched on, as it hardly comes in the category of philanthropic work. She has always shown herself to be in close touch with the pulse of national sentiment. Without this peculiar insight and ready sympathy, neither her prominent position, nor her eloquent pen, would have availed to give expression as she often has done to sentiments and desires, which, from time to time, were awakened in the hearts of the people.

A single instance may be given of this striking of the chord of popular feeling, by quoting a letter from *The Times*, in which the Baroness gave true and noble utterance to the wide-spread and indignant demand, that an effort should be made to rescue Gordon, who had been abandoned.

"I ask for a little space to make known through *The Times* the communications, or rather the entreaties, I have received from many personally unknown to me, to aid in organizing by public subscription a volunteer movement to attempt to relieve General Gordon. My correspondents are poor, but they offer to entrust to me all they can afford of their small means, and to raise their voices in unison with their wealthier fellow-countrymen against a base surrender of the nation's good faith and honor, as well as of a gallant and Christian life—a surrender which has united in a common indignation the French workman of Lyons, who offers you his twenty francs, with the English lady who, it is stated, has promised five thousand pounds for Gordon's defense. A Gordon Rescue Fund would have been started ere this had a rallying point been found upon

which the country could have concentrated its efforts. Had the Lord
Mayor felt he could convene a meeting, or had you, sir, felt it competent to undertake such a responsibility, a popular movement might by
this time have assumed a substantive
form. But no such organization was
effected. Now that General Gordon's
own statement of his position has been
unearthed, it would seem difficult to
point out from what direction an independent effort could be best guided to
assist him. General Gordon looks to
the Equator as his only point of refuge,
and Providence may shield him along
that wonderful and dangerous path.
Those in England who know what that
journey must be, and those who do
not, will alike feel with bitterness of
heart that it was not to England he
turned for hope in his abandonment.
Unlike the garrison at Sinkat, who, to
the last, would not believe they were to
die betrayed and deserted, General

Gordon recognizes his position—that
he is left single-handed to fight his
own battle; whether his generous im-
pulses toward those who have trusted
him in Khartoum will allow him to
adopt the only means of escape, or
will keep him there till the moment
when, to use his own words, he 'will
not be taken alive,' we cannot tell.
At least he makes no mistake now as
to the situation in which he has been
left.

"But if the voice of the people at
large could penetrate the deadly silence of Khartoum, Gordon would
know that the English nation, unrepre-
sented as it may have been through its
ordinary channels, had sprung to its
feet, and, moved by a spirit akin to his
own, was eager to strike a blow on its
own account on behalf of a man sent
out in his country's name.

"I have felt bound to make public
the evidences of this feeling which
have come under my observation.

Doubtless many others have received similar communications, and not only as a personal friend of General Gordon, but for the sake of the national honor, I would venture to express a hope that some record of this should be kept. For, although neither for us nor for him, if he be spared, can any movement for his personal safety wipe out what he justly terms the 'indelible disgrace' of abandoning the garrisons, we, the people, have never assented to an inscrutable policy of repudiation, and it must be some consolation to have recorded, by these emphatic proofs, the deep and wide-spread sympathy which has so stirred the national spirit."

One letter, as typical of hundreds of others, which this stirring appeal called forth, may be quoted :

"MADAM : It is not the first time by many that you have spoken to the world the thoughts that were burning in thousands of hearts, but for this

13

morning's letter to *The Times,* every
man and woman who loves England
surely owes you the poor tribute of
personal thanks. General Gordon's
life, noble as it is, would be, comparatively speaking, a slight thing were
not the nation's honor bound up with
it. It may be too late to avert 'indelible disgrace,' but let it be recorded
as you rightly propose, that the people
did not altogether acquiesce in its
shame. The women of England are,
at least, stirred by no party politics in
this matter. Few can follow one
splendid example and offer thousands,
but many a woman has been hoping
day by day to send her few hoarded
pounds to a 'Gordon Rescue Fund.'"

The Baroness provided funds for
Sir Henry James' topographical Survey
of Jerusalem, and offered to reinstate
the Aqueducts of Solomon to render
more certain the regular supply of
water to the capital of Christendom.

In Africa she provided a cotton gin to the mission of Abeokeuta, a simple act of well directed benevolence fruitful of great results. The Egban, of a much more enterprising nature than his neighbor the Fantee, seized his opportunity, and a special correspondent writing from the Gold Coast, at a later date, said, "Since the Baroness Burdett-Coutts first gave a cotton gin to the Missions at Abeokeuta, the cotton trade, which is almost entirely in the hands of the natives, has wonderfully increased, the approximate yearly export being upwards of ten thousand bales."

Societies for the protection of the aborigines were started at her suggestion in Australia; she has written and spoken against the Slave Trade in Africa, and planted the Church of England in several of our Colonies. In her beautiful grounds at Holly Lodge, Highgate, she has entertained most of the representative bodies who have visited England from abroad, including the Belgian Volunteers in 1867, when she gave a dinner to two thousand five hundred guests; the Delegates of the Chambers of Commerce of the world; Representatives of the Colonies and India; the members of the Medical, and of the Hygienic Congresses; and the American Civil Engineers. And lastly mention may be made of the assistance she has afforded to the Polish veterans, of whom a few still remain in London, who took part in the final struggle for the liberty of Poland in 1830-1.

CONCLUSION.

SUCH are some of the better known and public acts of a long lifetime; but it may be added that every day during all that period, the post has brought to her dozens of appeals from individuals, some asking for a few shillings, some asking the means of proving at law the right to a peerage! These letters have come to her from persons in every rank of society. Many no doubt were not deserving of attention; but among the others was many a touching case of real sorrow and distress, and some of the letters came from the unfortunate victims of fantastic combinations of circumstances such as fiction has hardly dreamed of.

The queenly generosity by which the work described in these pages was prompted and supported, has been recognized all the world over, and has frequently received official acknowledgement. The Baroness has received the freedom of the cities of London, Manchester, and Edinburgh. As already related, she has been given by the Sultan the Orders of the Medjidiyeh and the Shafakat. On hearing that the cordon of the former had been worn by the Baroness at an English official reception, his Majesty sent to her ladyship through Hobart Pasha the special message that, "His Majesty the Sultan is much pleased to count you among his sincere and kind friends."

In 1871 amid universal approval, the Queen conferred on Miss Burdett-Coutts the signal honor of a peerage of the United Kingdom, under the title of the Baroness Burdett-Coutts. This is the only instance of a woman having been raised to the peerage in recognition of her own life and deeds, and independently of any other consideration

These are some of the official and formal tributes which the Baroness has received, but others equally prized are those which have so often arisen spontaneously from the hearts of the people, the fervent "God bless you" of the Newcastle miners, the flowers with which the village street has been hastily carpeted at the news of her coming, the hill-side fires with which she was welcomed by the Irish peasants. Mr. Julian Young narrates how, in 1868, when the Reform procession occupied nearly three hours in passing the well-known house at the corner of Stratton Street, London, Miss Burdett-Coutts was recognized. "In one instant a shout was raised, not only by the artisan and laboring classes that formed the procession, but by the bystanders who lined the thoroughfare. For upwards of two hours and a half the air rang with reiterated huzzas, huzzas unanimous and heartfelt as if representing a national feeling." Similar demon-

strations have been witnessed more
than once since that time, and are one
of many tokens of the unique position
that the Baroness has for ever secured
to herself in the hearts of the people.

INDEX.

For EU product safety concerns, contact us at Calle de José Abascal, 56–1°,
28003 Madrid, Spain or eugpsr@cambridge.org.

 www.ingramcontent.com/pod-product-compliance
Ingram Content Group UK Ltd.
Pitfield, Milton Keynes, MK11 3LW, UK
UKHW012346130625
459647UK00009B/571